John Bracegirdle's
Psychopharmacon

ΜΕΔΙΕVAL & RENAISSANCE

TEXTS & STUDIES

VOLUME 200

John Bracegirdle's
Psychopharmacon

A Translation of Boethius'

De Consolatione Philosophiae

(MS BL Additional 11401)

Edited by

Noel Harold Kaylor, Jr. & Jason Edward Streed

Arizona Center for Medieval and Renaissance Studies
Tempe, Arizona
1999

Library of Congress Cataloging-in-Publication Data

Bracegirdle, John, d. 1614.
    [Psychopharmacon]
    John Bracegirdle's Psychopharmacon : a translation of Boethius' De consolatione philosophiae (MS BL additional 11401) / edited by Noel Harold Kaylor, Jr. & Jason Edward Streed.
       p. cm. — (Medieval & Renaissance Texts & Studies ; v. 200)
    Includes bibliographical references (p.).
    ISBN 0-86698-242-6 (alk. paper)
    1. Philosophy and religion—Poetry. 2. Happiness—Poetry. I. Boethius, d. 524. De consolatione philosophiae. II. Kaylor, Noel Harold, 1946- . III. Streed, Jason Edward, 1971- . IV. Title. V. Series: Medieval & Renaissance Texts & Studies (Series) ; v. 200.
    PR2214.B17P78 1999
    100—dc21   98–52871
                                               CIP

∞

This book is made to last.
It is set in Garamond,
smythe-sewn and printed on acid-free paper
to library specifications.

Printed in the United States of America

For

Derek and Rosemary,

with

gratitude and affection

Table of Contents

Acknowledgments

The editors would to thank the librarians at the British Library and the archivists in its manuscript room for their active assistance during the several years required in transcribing and editing MS BL Additional 11401. They have been most gracious in providing information on the history of the manuscript and the biographies of its translator and owners.

We are greatly indebted to Dr. Mario A. Di Cesare for his patience and lucid advice concerning every aspect of the preparation of this edition of John Bracegirdle's *Psychopharmacon*. Without his continued encouragement, we might never have brought this project to completion.

Finally, the editors must acknowledge the encouragement of their respective family members, Alliegordon Kaylor and Candy Streed, whose active support and personal sacrifice of time have made the editing of this manuscript possible.

Introduction

I
MS BL ADDITIONAL 11401

Early Critical References to the Translation

The *Dictionary of National Biography* notes that one John Bracegirdle produced a translation of Boethius' *De Consolatione Philosophiae*, the *Psychopharmacon*, that bears a very lengthy subtitle: *The Mindes Medicine or the Phisicke of Philosophie, contained in five bookes, called the Consolation of Philosophie, compiled by Anicius, Manlius Torquatus Severinus Boethius, in the Time of His Exile and Proscription.*[1] This entry in the *DNB* derives from an earlier entry in the *Athenae Cantabrigienses*, similar in phrasing, which also credits John Bracegirdle with the authorship of the *Psychopharmacon*.[2]

Bracegirdle's translation is a fairly accurate English rendering of the Latin *Consolatio*, with Latin prose passages translated into blank verse and Latin meters into a variety of metrical forms. The first critical mention of the translation is found in Thomas Warton's *History of English Poetry* of 1871.[3] In a short article of 1892 by Ewald Flügel,[4] some short extracts from the translation appear, offering for the first time a printed indication of Bracegirdle's poetic abilities. Concerning Bracegirdle's blank verse, Flügel says:

> ... certain parts of the translation attain a full poetic power and elegance which permits us to see in Bracegirdle a by-no-means

---

[1] *Dictionary of National Biography*, "John Bracegirdle," vol. 6, ed. Sidney Lee (London: Smith, Elder, & Co., 1899), 142.

[2] *Athenae Cantabrigienses*, vol. 2, *1586–1609*, ed. Charles Henry Cooper and Thompson Cooper (Cambridge: Deighton, Bell, & Co., 1861), 430.

[3] Thomas Warton, *History of English Poetry from the Twelfth to the Sixteenth Century*, vol. 3, ed. W.C. Hazlitt (London: 1871; repr. Hildesheim: Georg Olms, 1968), 38–40.

[4] Ewald Flügel, "Kleinere Mitteilungen aus Handschriften," *Anglia* 14 (1892): 499–501.

insignificant Elizabethan poet.[5] [editors' translation from the German]

Friedrich Fehlauer cites these notices by Warton and Flügel in his dissertation of 1908,[6] in which he discusses the extant *Consolatio* translations into English to about 1800 and briefly mentions some of the more recent ones. He does not claim to have perused the *Psychopharmacon* itself, but he notes its existence among the other English translations. In 1992, a note on the Bracegirdle translation appeared in *The Medieval Consolation of Philosophy: An Annotated Bibliography*, in a section devoted to Chaucer's *Consolatio* translation, the *Boece*.[7]

Ownership of the Manuscript

MS BL Additional 11401, the unique manuscript containing John Bracegirdle's translation, was produced about 1602, and it was probably presented to Thomas Sackville, the translator's patron, in or shortly after that year. At some point, however, it must have been sold by the Sackville estate, because it next appears in the record when it was purchased by the British Museum on July 14, 1838, from Thomas Rodd, the younger, a bookseller at Covent Garden, who had taken over the family's London business from his father in 1821. The manuscript remains today in the collection of the British Library.

Description of the Manuscript

The manuscript's cover is of stiff vellum, enclosing paper pages, and it cannot be dated accurately. Watermarks on the manuscript's paper pages, however, permit their dating.[8] The paper for the text of the translation itself was made near Rouen about 1575; paper for three blank pages bound in at the front and at the back of the inscribed text were made in Likhatscheff about 1600; two blank pages that are bound into the manuscript inside the front and back covers, as "cover sheets or end

---

[5] Flügel, "Kleinere Mitteilungen," 501.

[6] Friedrich Fehlauer, "Die englischen Übersetzungen von Boethius' De Consolatione Philosophiae," Ph.D. diss., Albertus-Universität zu Königsberg, 1908 (Königsberg: Hartungsche Buchdruckerei, 1908).

[7] Noel Harold Kaylor, Jr., *The Medieval Consolation of Philosophy: An Annotated Bibliography*, Garland Medieval Bibliographies, no. 7 (New York: Garland Publishing, Inc., 1992).

[8] C.M. Briquet, *Les Filigranes: Dictionnaire Historique des Marques du Papier*, second edition, vol. 4 (Leipzig: Verlag von Karl W. Hiersenam, 1923), entry numbers 12693 and 12783.

papers," are of more recent origin. The *Psychopharmacon*, transcribed onto such fine, imported paper, was obviously produced as an elegant gift for Thomas Sackville, to whom the work is dedicated, "as a small token of [Bracegirdle's] loyal affection and gratitude."

The pages of the manuscript are 20 x 30.5 cm, and the vellum covers are slightly wider. The translation *per se* comprises sixty-two pages (124 sides) inscribed front and back, ending on page 62 *verso*, which is blank on its *verso* side. Preceding the translation, there are, first, the two cover sheets; then, the three blank sheets produced about 1600; a title page, later numbered in pencil as "1," left blank on its *verso* side; Bracegirdle's Dedication, later numbered in pencil as "2," also left blank on its *verso* side; and then five slightly wider sheets, folded at the center, with their outer edges then folded inward toward each other (a total of three parallel folds per sheet) so that the folded width of each of these inserts conforms to the 20 cm width of the other manuscript pages. These five inserted, double pages (numbered in pencil as pages "3" through "12") have been glued along the outer edges of their central creases to bound pages in the manuscript that had been cut down to a width of one centimeter for this purpose. When opened, each of these five fold-out pages reveals an outline or flow-chart summarizing the content of one of the five books of the *Consolatio*. The translation itself then follows, with its first page numbered in pencil as "13." At the back of the translation, there are three blank pages, corresponding to the three at the front, and two cover sheets, also corresponding to sheets at the front.

Peculiarities of the Manuscript

The translation is transcribed by at least two hands, one having produced the blank-verse passages (into which the Boethian prose passages are translated) and another having produced the various rubrics, the Boethian meters (all of which appear in italic), and the frequent italicized words introduced into the blank-verse passages. A third hand, possibly that of Bracegirdle himself, produced the Dedication to Thomas Sackville, the Earl of Dorset, which prefaces the translation, and Bracegirdle's signature (John Bracegirdle, Bacheler in Divinity), is inscribed at the bottom of this Dedication. Evidence signaling the collaboration of two amanuenses (one for non-italic and another for italic elements) is of several distinct varieties. First, certain minor but fairly consistent orthographic practices distinguish the two hands. Second, some rubrics are otherwise inexplicably mislabeled or omitted altogether. Third, within the blank-verse passages, italicized words sometimes vary in size and position relative to the non-italicized words, indicating that they were probably inserted later into spaces left available by the blank-verse hand. As an example of the confusion potential in this procedure, in Book III, Prose 8, line 1, the blank-verse scribe wrote the first two letters of the final word of that verse, the *be* of *beatitude*, but noticing his error, he crossed out the letters; the correctly italicized word was inscribed thereafter in the italic hand. The italicized words, passages, and meters in the manuscript are retained in this edition because they do influence a reading of the translation.

The ink used in the Bracegirdle signature is darker than that used by the scribes of the translation, but it occasionally appears in short, correctional over-writes within the work, suggesting that the translator probably checked the final transcription himself. There are two systems of pagination in the manuscript: one, in the ink of the text, numbering the first page of the translation itself as "1" (and it is this original pagination that we record in this edition); another, in pencil, from a later date, numbering Bracegirdle's title page as "1" and the first page of the translation as "13." The "ink pagination" appears centered at the top of each inscribed *recto* page. The "pencil pagination" appears in the upper right corner of the inscribed *recto* pages. Each inscribed page in the manuscript normally ends with a reader's prompt, which anticipates the first few words found at the beginning of the following page. These are written in the hand of the passage that follows, either in the non-italic or italic hand. Occasionally, prompts are missing, and the omission most often occurs when the opening verse of the following page begins the translation of a new prose (non-italic) or meter (italic) passage, suggesting that the succeeding amanuensis had failed to notice the missing prompt on the previous page upon returning to work. If there had been but one amanuensis, the prompt probably would have been inscribed before the page was turned. The translations of all five books of the *Consolatio* begin on a fresh page of the manuscript. The single exception to this practice occurs with Book III, introduced rather unceremoniously after Book II, Meter 8, at the bottom of 19 *verso*. Corrections of words, phrases, and even of whole verses, appear throughout the manuscript, but in general, the scribal work demonstrates a conscientious effort to present Bracegirdle's translation in an appropriately attractive, clear, and readable transcription.

Bracegirdle's Prosody

On one of the blank pages at the front of Bracegirdle's *Psychophar-*

macon is found the following notice, which was glued into the manuscript sometime after 1838:

> This is an autograph, and unpublished. It is dedicated to the Earl of Dorset (Sackville, the poet) and is written in a very beautiful hand. The interest and curiosity of the manuscript consists in the whole of the prose of Boethius being rendered into blank verse, exhibiting the longest specimen of that kind then existing in the English language. The metres are translated into different kinds of English verse, some of them entirely new, rhyming hexametres, pentametres, &c. The performance is evidently that of a poet of no mean ability, and is done with great spirit and easy flow of versification.

Considering Bracegirdle's results, "performance" is indeed a fair description of the *Psychopharmacon*. Both the great number of verse forms and the "curiosity" of the blank verse place the work's form in the foreground, as though it were a field in which Bracegirdle sought to prove the range of his inventiveness and command of English prosody. The complete spectrum of his experimentation in verse form is catalogued in Appendix I of this edition. The variety of forms and meters Bracegirdle employs is impressive: among the work's thirty-nine meters are twenty-seven distinct stanzaic and metrical variations, and the most common stanza, the sestet, appears in seven different forms. Naturally, some meters are more successful than are others, and if a few approach failure, others do achieve an "easy flow of versification."

Bracegirdle's translations of certain meters into quantitative verse represent his least successful experiments in distinctive verse forms.[9] His translation begins, unfortunately, with one of these. The rendering of Boethius' opening meter, which Bracegirdle fashions in an odd combination of rhyming couplets and quantitative verse, gives little indication of the elegance and musicality he attains later, in the majority of his verse renderings.[10]

More satisfying are Bracegirdle's translations of meters into borrowed or invented forms. These range from the heroic couplets of Book

---

[9] Book I, Meter 1; Book II, Meter 7; Book V, Meter 5.

[10] See Derek Attridge, *Well-Weighted Syllables: Elizabethan Verse in Classical Meters* (Cambridge: Cambridge University Press, 1974). He argues, for example, that, during the Elizabethan period, *theories and rules* rather than *sound* guided many English experiments in classical meter (160). This observation might explain why Bracegirdle could place so awkward a verse in so strategic a position in his translation.

I, Meter 4, to the elaborately contrived stanzas of Book III, Meter 1. This latter meter exemplifies one of the peculiar forms Bracegirdle sometimes employs: it is a nonce form in ten lines, rhyming *abcdabcdee*, with an initial octave in iambic dimeter and a concluding couplet in iambic tetrameter, with interlaced rhyme, which creates a caesura in each verse. More familiar forms employed by Bracegirdle include: ottava rima (in the fashion of Ariosto and Spenser), which appears three times, and rime royal, in hexameters, which appears fittingly in the majestic Book III, Meter 9.

Generally, Bracegirdle handles his forms well, indicating special fondness and aptitude for stanzas that conclude in couplets or quatrains, which he often crafts into memorable or almost gnomic coinings. This predilection for creating memorable phrasing also is evidenced in his blank-verse renderings of Boethius' prose passages, in which Bracegirdle's innovative skills find their most successful expression. Blank verse first appears in English in Surrey's translation of Virgil's *Aeneid*, Books II and IV, published in 1557. Thereafter, outside of drama, blank verse appears only briefly, in obscure examples.[11] Whatever the merits of the blank verse experiments by Spenser, Gascoigne, Peele and others, nothing like Bracegirdle's extensive use of the form appeared in English until Milton perfected it several decades later, in his *Paradise Lost* of 1667.

II
THE HISTORICAL RECORD

John Bracegirdle

The *Dictionary of National Biography* further states that John Bracegirdle "is *supposed* [editors' italics] to have been a son of John Bracegirdle, who was vicar of Stratford-upon-Avon from 1560 to 1569."[12] If this were true, then the translator's father baptized William Shakespeare, and the future translator probably would have been acquainted with the future bard during his childhood, and they probably would have gone to school together. Concerning this vicar, who came to Stratford during a very eventful period of the English Reformation, F.E. Halliday says:

---

[11] See George K. Smart, "English Non-Dramatic Blank Verse in the Sixteenth Century," *Anglia* 61 (1937): 370–397. Smart does not mention Bracegirdle in this very thorough study.

[12] *DNB*, "John Bracegirdle," vol. 6, 142.

The Catholic vicar [at Stratford] was removed and replaced by the Protestant John Bretchgirdle, who re-introduced the Prayer Book of Edward VI and re-organized the services according to the rules laid down by Elizabeth. No doubt there were many Catholics who easily accommodated themselves to the new dispensation, but there were zealots like the Cloptons, Reynoldses and Lanes who refused to attend church and preferred to pay the monthly fine for their recusancy. They were in a minority, however, for Stratford was becoming increasingly Protestant . . .[13]

However, one of Shakespeare's biographers, S. Schoenbaum, adds this rather unpromising information on the life of John Bretchgirdle, the supposed father of the translator of Boethius: "He was unmarried—a sister, perhaps two sisters, kept house for him . . ."[14] This statement is substantiated by such historical documents as Bretchgirdle's will,[15] and it renders unacceptable the information given in the *DNB*.

The volume of the *Athenae Cantabrigienses*, noted above as the source of information later printed in the *DNB*, indicates that one John Brasgirdle or Bracegirdle (author of the *Psychopharmacon*) was matriculated as sizar of Queen's College, Cambridge, in December of 1588. He received his B.A. in 1592, his M.A. in 1595, and his B.D. in 1602. The reference further states that "John Bracegirdle . . . is *supposed* [editors' italics] to have been a son [of a man] of the same name who was vicar of Stratford-upon-Avon from 1560–1569." In all probability, this is the original supposition that has generated all subsequent references to Bracegirdle's possible Stratford origin. A later catalog of Cambridge graduates, the *Alumni Cantabrigienses*, omits the notice concerning his Stratford birth, stating rather that John Bracegirdle was born in Cheshire.[16] This later reference also states that the *Consolatio* translator was buried at Rye on February 8, 1614 (thus, John Bracegirdle preceded William Shakespeare in death by approximately two years).

A similarity with the name of the vicar of Stratford and congruity of chronology with the bard of Stratford would indicate a connection with the vicar, John Bretchgirdle, but the historical documents do not.

---

[13] F.E. Halliday, *Shakespeare* (New York: Thomas Yoseloff, 1961), 19.

[14] S. Schoenbaum, *William Shakespeare: A Compact Documentary Life* (New York: Oxford University Press, 1977), 23.

[15] See Edgar I Fripp, "John Brownsword: Poet and Schoolmaster at Stratford-upon-Avon," *Hibbert Journal* (1921): 551–564.

[16] *Alumni Cantabrigienses*, John Venn and J.A. Venn, eds., Part I (to 1751), vol. 1 (Cambridge: Cambridge University Press, 1922), 208.

§

John Bracegirdle's career as a clergyman began May 14, 1598, when he was ordained a priest. He became rector of St. John's-sub-Castro at Lewes in 1598 and then rector of St. Thomas-in-the-Cliff in 1599. He was appointed vicar of Rye in 1602 and eventually vicar of Peasmarsh in 1606.[17] For his *Consolatio* translation, Bracegirdle's appointment to the vicarage of Rye in 1602 is of primary importance, and its documentation in the bishop's record, held today in the church archive at Chichester, states that Bracegirdle was presented for this position by Thomas Sackville, lord Buckhurst, on July 12 of that year.[18] Bracegirdle dedicated his translation of the *Consolatio* to Thomas Sackville, High Treasurer of England, in 1602 or sometime shortly thereafter. In his Dedication, Bracegirdle states that he had benefited from reading the Boethian work during difficult times and he offers it to the High Treasurer in gratitude for his "favors and most ample benefit," which were granted "freely and often." The presentation for his Rye appointment establishes at least one basis for Bracegirdle's statement of gratitude to Sackville.

The translation itself represents an honorable effort at rendering into English both the form and the content of one of the major works of late Antiquity. It is a fitting gift for a patron whose creative and intellectual interests are as well documented as Sackville's are.

§

The *Athenae Cantabrigienses* further notes that one John Bracegirdle, perhaps the son of the *Consolatio* translator, received his B.A. at Trinity College in 1629 and his M.A. in 1632.[19] In the case of this entry, the exactness of the names and the appropriateness of the dates lend credence to the speculation it promotes.

Bracegirdle's Patron: Thomas Sackville
Concerning Thomas Sackville, we know much. He was the only son of Sir Richard Sackville, born at Buckhurst, Sussex, in 1536. His career divides into two parts: as a young man, he devoted his attention to literature, but as an adult, he found his calling in politics.

---

[17] *Alumni Cantabrigienses*, vol. 1, 208.
[18] Diocese of Chichester, Record of the Bishop, Ep 1 / 1 / 8A, folio 17v–18r.
[19] *Athenae Cantabrigienses*, vol. 2, 430.

In the mid-1550s, he hoped to write a poem based on Lydgate's *Fall of Princes*.

> The poet was to describe his descent into the infernal regions after the manner of Virgil and Dante, and to recount the lives of those dwellers there who, having distinguished themselves in English history, had come to untimely ends. Sackville prepared a poetical preface which he called an "Introduction." Here "Sorrow" guides the narrator through Hades, and after the poet has held converse with the shades of the heroes of antiquity he meets the ghost of Henry Stafford, duke of Buckingham, who recites to him his tragic story.[20]

Sackville's early literary aspirations thus were ambitious. Although his adaptation of the *Fall of Princes* was never completed, his "Introduction" and the "Complaint of the Duke of Buckingham" from this fragmentary work were eventually incorporated into the second volume of *A Myrroure for Magistrates*, by Richard Baldwin and George Ferrers, which appeared in 1563. In English literary history, Thomas Sackville is probably most renowned for his work with Thomas Norton on *Gorboduc*, which is "perhaps the earliest classical tragedy in England" and "presented before Queen Elizabeth at Whitehall on January 18, 1562."[21]

Sackville's political career developed during the reign of Elizabeth I. On 17 March 1563, he conveyed a message from parliament to the queen. The queen recognized his kinship with her—his father was Anne Boleyn's first cousin—and she showed much liking for him, ordering him to be in continual attendance on her.[22] Under Elizabeth, Sackville made several diplomatic journeys and held various offices. Particularly noteworthy is the following: "In December 1588 he was appointed a commissioner for ecclesiastical causes."[23] Sackville's holding this office could explain why he became John Bracegirdle's patron.

> It was ten years later [ten years after 1588] that Sackville was awarded his highest political office.

> In August 1598 Lord-treasurer Burghley died, and court

---

[20] *DNB*, "Sackville," vol. 17, 586.

[21] David Bevington, *The Complete Works of Shakespeare*, 4th ed. (New York: Harper-Collins, 1992), xxxviii.

[22] *DNB*, "Sackville," vol. 17, 587.

[23] *DNB*, "Sackville," vol. 17, 587.

gossip at once nominated Buckhurst to the vacant post (Chamberlain, *Letters*, pp. 31, 37); but it was not until 19 May 1599 that he was installed in the office of treasurer.[24]

§

In his political career, Thomas Sackville survived the death of Elizabeth I, maintaining political favor into the early years of the Jacobean age.

III
THE EARLY EUROPEAN TRADITION
OF *CONSOLATIO* TRANSLATIONS

The European tradition of vernacular translations of Boethius' *De Consolatione Philosophiae* begins in Britain ca. 899 with the appearance of Alfred the Great's rendering of the Latin work into Old English. The entire Latin text was translated into prose, but somewhat later the Latin verses (except for nine meters) were translated separately into Old English alliterative verse.[25] The *Consolatio* translation was part of Alfred's library of basic texts for the education of his subjects.

On the Continent, about the year 1000, Notker Labeo of St. Gall translated the *Consolatio* into Old High German.[26] His interlinear rendering is thought to have been used in the instruction of Latin at the monastery school of St. Gall. From later periods, both Middle High German and Early Modern German translations either survive or are attested.

The most extensive interest in translating the *Consolatio* into a European vernacular is found in France. At least thirteen medieval translations, of varied quality and affiliation, date from the thirteenth, fourteenth, and fifteenth centuries.[27] Among these is one by Jean de Meun, who also wrote the famous thirteenth-century continuation of

---

[24] *DNB*, "Sackville," vol. 17, 588.

[25] Walter John Sedgefield, ed., *King Alfred's Old English Version of Boethius'* De Consolatione Philosophiae (1899; repr. Darmstadt: Wissenschaft-liche Buchstellschaft, 1968).

[26] Paul Piper, ed., *Die Schriften Notkers und seiner Schule*, Germanischer Bücherschatz, No. 8–? (Freiburg und Tübingen: Akademische Verlags-buchhandlung von J.C.B. Mohr, 1883).

[27] See Kaylor, *The Medieval Consolation of Philosophy*.

Guillaume de Lorris' unfinished *Roman de la rose*.[28]

During the Middle English period, Geoffrey Chaucer consulted Jean de Meun's French translation of the *Consolatio* when he himself translated Boethius' last work.[29] Chaucer's translation survives in an incunabulum edition, published by Caxton about 1478, as well as in eleven manuscripts or manuscript fragments. Chaucer's translation, the *Boece* of about 1380, is entirely in prose. Working in the early fifteenth century, an anonymous adapter of Boethius produced an unusual all-prose revision of *Consolatio*, Book I. It has been referred to as a translation by some scholars,[30] but upon closer examination, it proves to be a reworking of Chaucer's *Boece*, Book I, interspersed with commentary of a very idiosyncratic nature.[31] In 1410, John Walton, working under the patronage of Lady Elizabeth Berkeley, produced an all-verse rendering of the Boethian work.[32] Consulting a Latin manuscript, he cast Chaucer's prose into English verse, partly in rime royal and partly in eight-line stanzas, both of which Chaucer also had used successfully. Walton's translation, too, appeared in an incunabulum edition.

The next known English translation of the *Consolatio* was the work of Queen Elizabeth I. She rendered the Latin prose into English prose and the Latin verse into English verse in 1593, but the translation remained in manuscript form until an edition was published in 1899.[33] John Bracegirdle's translation followed next, about 1602, and it has remained heretofore unpublished. Neither Elizabeth I nor John Bracegirdle appear to have consulted any previously existing vernacular renderings of the *Consolatio* as they prepared their translations. Each work represents an independent effort at rendering both the form and content of Boethius' work into Early Modern English. This edition of Bracegirdle's translation completes the work of editing all known English *Consolatio* translations of the Middle Ages and Renaissance.

---

[28] Venceslas Louis Dedeck-Héry, "Boethius' *De Consolatione* by Jean de Meun," *Medieaval Studies* 14 (1952): 165–275.

[29] Larry D. Benson, ed., *The Riverside Chaucer*, 3rd ed. (Boston: Houghton Mifflin, 1987).

[30] See Mark Liddel, "Letter," *Academy*, 7 March 1896; Fehlauer, "Die englischen Übersetzungen."

[31] Noel Harold Kaylor, Jr., Jason Edward Streed, and William H. Watts, "The Boke of Coumfort," *Carmina Philosophiae* 2 (1993): 55–104.

[32] Mark Science, ed., *Boethius*: De Consolatione Philosophiae, John Walton, trans., Early English Text Society, no. 170 (London: Oxford University Press, 1927).

[33] Caroline Pemberton, ed., *Queen Elizabeth's Englishings of Boethius, De Consolatione Philosophiae; Plutarch, De Curiositate; Horace, De Arte Poetica (part)*, Early English Text Society, No. 113 (London: Kegan Paul, Trench, Trübner and Co., 1899).

IV
HYPOTHESES ON BRACEGIRDLE'S
CHOICE OF A TEXT FOR HIS PATRON

Elizabeth I was a woman of considerable learning: among her many other accomplishments, she had full mastery of French and Latin, and she had a reasonable command of Italian and Greek. Even as monarch she found the time to translate certain Latin works herself. These intellectual exercises include her translation of Boethius' *Consolatio*, which she produced in 1593. It is said that she made this particular translation in an effort to console herself over the conversion of Henry of Navarre to Catholicism; he had converted from Protestantism, of course, so that he could become Henry IV, Catholic King of France.[34]

Boethius' last and most renowned work was not unknown in Renaissance England. As pointed out above, the English tradition of *Consolatio* translations was already established through the renderings by Alfred and by Chaucer particularly. By 1602, when Sackville presented Bracegirdle for the vicarage of Rye, it may also have been generally known, at least in court circles, that Queen Elizabeth I herself had translated the *Consolatio*. If Bracegirdle had finished his own translation before 1603, the year in which the Queen died, and this is indeed probable, it might have been so that Sackville could have had his own version of the text in English, so that he would have been more fully conversant with the literature of consolation that the sovereign had translated as she was approaching her seventieth year. This theory might also explain why the translation fell into almost complete obscurity: after 1603, Sackville's intellectual and political interests would have turned in other directions. However, this theory also seems to require that the suggestion of the gift of a *Consolatio* translation would have originated in some way from Sackville.

It is also possible that Bracegirdle offered his translation of Boethius' last work as a lamentable story similar to those that had interested Sackville in his youth. The tragic (or *casus*) element that is inherent in the *Consolatio* might then lie behind the work's appeal to Sackville, who was also responsible for writing at least the last two acts of *Gorboduc* (a tragedy and the first English play in blank verse). Bracegirdle probably would have been aware of his patron's own literary endeavors in dramatic tragedy. If, as Bracegirdle seems to suggest at one point in his

---

[34] See Pemberton, *Queen Elizabeth's Englishings*.

Dedication, he had already been a student of the *Consolatio* for some time, then the choice of texts might have originated with the translator, who could see grounds in Boethius for intellectual and literary kinship with his patron.

Ultimately, the question of why Bracegirdle chose to translate the *Consolatio* and no other work for his patron remains unanswerable. However, his rendering the Latin original into the decorous blank verse and various metrical forms he chose, rather than into prose, indicates that he was interested in demonstrating his own agility in producing English prosody, as well as in presenting in English the message of consolation found in the Boethian work. The general quality of Bracegirdle's translation and prosody indicate that he did not work in haste; Bracegirdle's rendering has all the appearance of resulting from a labor of love, for the *Consolatio*, on the one hand, and for the writing of verses, on the other.

V

EDITORIAL PRACTICE AND NOTATION

This edition of Bracegirdle's *Psychopharmacon* retains as many of the formal features of MS BL Additional 11401 as possible in a semi-diplomatic transcription of the manuscript. The sometimes idiosyncratic orthography of the scribes is maintained, except where confusion could result, and these few instances in which emendations seemed advisable are noted; expanded abbreviations are enclosed in brackets, but letters superscripted in the manuscript are superscripted in the edition. For convenience of reference, the lines of each prose and meter passage are numbered separately. Bracegirdle's Dedication comprises thirty lines of prose on one page of the manuscript. Whereas the original lineation in the verse and blank-verse passages has been carefully preserved throughout this edition, it has not been retained in this unique prose passage. In the manuscript, the original page numbers appear at the head of each *recto* page of the translation; in order not to disrupt the flow of text unnecessarily, we have moved these numbers back to the end of the last line of verse at the bottom of the previous page.

John Bracegirdle is generally an excellent versifier. However, lines that are metrically short occasionally appear. On the other hand, with some frequency, unaccented endings, elided syllables, and seemingly superfluous words also appear, yielding metrically long lines. No at-

tempt has been made in this edition to emend these seeming inconsisten-
cies (except in two instances, one in Book IV and another in Book V, in
which the Latin text suggests an acceptable emendation), and they
present no obstacle in appreciating the translation.

For convenience, some unusual words are defined in Appendix II:
Selective Glossary. Each occurrence of these words is indicated in the
edited text with a raised circle (for example: *bewray*°). Indications of
non-textual elements, such as the seal of the British Museum, which has
been stamped in red on several pages of the manuscript, have been
omitted without documentation.

John Bracegirdle's
Psychopharmacon

Psychopharmacon.
The Mindes Medicine, *or the*
Phisicke of Philosophie, *contained*
in five bookes,. called the Consolation of
Philosophie, compiled by Anicius, ~
Manlius Torquatus Seve//
rinus Boethius, *in the*
time of his exile and
proscription.

To the Right Honorable my singuler
   good Lord the Earl of Dorsett, Lord
     high Treasurer of England, et:

Right Honorable:[1] the Romayne usage,[2] that none presum'd to approach to any of sort more eminent, w[th]out some significac[i]on of their
love, by some rare guift hath[3] mooved me to p[re]sume to p[re]sent this
small token of my loyall affection, and gratitude, unto yo[ur] hono[ur].
Wherein, though I may seeme rather guiltie of impudence[4] then mynde-
full of my imbecillity[5] and obscuritie in attempting to offer this Trala-
c[i]on to yo[ur] worthiest self, of *Divine Boecius*: yet notw[th]standing[,][6]
yo[ur] hono[urs] favors, and most ample benefitte, to mee freely, and
often collated, have emboldened mee to undertake the one, [and] y[e]
benefitt w[ch] I have often sucked in difficulties from this worke, hath
urged mee, long since, to undertake y[e] other. Who more fitt or able to
iudge of this worke, then yo[ur] hono[ur]? Who have heretofore most
gravely [and] prudently taken paynes therein?[7] What worke more
availeable to all Estates, to p[er]swade the mynde to calme contentment
in y[e] sturdy stormes of all crossing chaunges, then this Author? Breefly
the quiett establishing of my bodily estate proceedeth by meanes of
yo[ur] hono[ur], and my myndes establishm[ent] by meanes of this
author. Yf any obiect, I ought not imploye myself so much in *Philosophie*, [and] *Poetrie*: I answere this booke contayneth excellent grounds of
Divinitie. But I write this privately, to signifie my obedience [and]
thanckfullnes, not to satisfie y[e] Curious, most humbly beseeching yo[ur]
honorable acceptance hereof, w[ch] is all that I desire, [and] more then

---

[1] **Right Honorable:]** Right Honorable, *MS*
[2] usage,] use *MS*
[3] hath] hath, *MS*
[4] impudence] impudence, *MS*
[5] imbecillity] imbecillity, *MS*
[6] notw[th]standing[,]] notw[th]standing *MS*
[7] therein?] therein. *MS*

sufficient recompence for my poore labors, who rest in all duetifull affecc[i]on at yo[ur] hono[urs] commaundement and service, to expresse greater meanes of gratefull remembrance of yo[ur] hono[urs] benefitte, whensoever abilitie, [and] oportunity shal be offered. In the meane season, I most humbly, [and] in hartiest prayer commend yo[ur] hono[ur], my right honorable Lady, yo[ur] honorable progeny, and family, to y[e] blessed protection of the Almightie *Fountaine* of eternall felicitie, in whome I rest,

Your Honors servant at
commaund,

John Bracegirdle · *Bacheler*
in Divinity ·

THE · PHYSICKE · OF · PHILOSOPHIE.[1] /
contained in five bookes, compiled by Anicius
Manlius Torquatus Severinus
Boethius, touching the consolation
of Lady Philosophie in the
tyme of his banishment.

The first booke expressing the signes,
and causes of Boethius his sicknes. /

The first Meter ·
I, who did, in study late florishing, meditate mery verses,
In ditties tragicall, am, alas, constren'd to rehearse these. /
See, the rufull Muses do relate to me songes to be viewed,
And to lament miseries, wth teares, sory cheekes they be-dewed.
5 *Terror at all could never amaze them, or urge to relent them,*
But that alonge followinge me banished, only they went then.
These were a glory to youth many daies, when pleasure abounded,
Now they solace sely° daies, wth greife verie mightely wounded,
For very fast old age doth approach, wth labor, or ache spent,
10 *And miseries that I feele, compell horie heares, to be present.*
Such graie heares to my head, redy prest untimely be hasted,
And wrinckled skin, apace shivereth, on a weake body wasted.
Fortunate is mans death, so she spare men, in absolute yonge yeares,
And to release maladies, that abound, will not tarry longe teares.
15 *(Ah me, a wretch) to my suit very deafe no returne she replieth,*
Death cruel, eies miserable to close, very stoutly denieth.
While ficle fortune of old favoured, full treacherous in shiftes,
Deathes sorrowfull last howre, well neare had abandoned all giftes.
Now to sinister event, chance changed againe me betrayinge,

---

[1] *PHILOSOPHIE] PHILOSOPIE MS*

20   *Iniurious life, longe protracteth tyme by delayinge.*
      Why did ye my state, freinds, boast often aloft to be mounted?
      Farre from a state stablished, who so falles may truly be counted. /

                        Prose 1
      These things while I did wth my selfe record,
      And had wth penne, my pensive playrits displaied,
      A woman reverend, in semely shape,
      W^th ardent eies, peircinge beyond mans reach,
5   Over my head appeared then to stand,
      Of lively coulour, and unwasted strength,
      Allthough to be so full of daies she seemed,
      That of this age to be, none would have deemed.
      Her stature allwaies was not of one height,
10   Somtyme no taller then a common man,
      To touch the sky sometyme *her* head did seeme,
      Who when *her* head *she* did mount upp on highe,
      Above mans sight *she* past the azure sky.
      Her garments were wth finest threeds compact,   [1 v]
15   W^th matter intricate, and *art* exact.
      These garments *she*, (as afterward *she* sayd)
      Compiled of *her* selfe, whose outward *showe*
      By negligence of man in former daies,
      Darknes, like smoked pictures, had obscur'd.
20   In nether² hemme wherof .*P.* did appeare,
      In the upper part, *T.* was embroydered,
      Betwen wch le[tt]res, certaine stepes were wrought
      Like staiers compact, whereby from *P.* belowe,
      To *T.* above, wth ease one might ascend.
25   Yet was this garment rent by violence
      Of some, who, what they could purloine, did take.
      In *her* right hand some bookes *she* also bare,
      A septer, in *her* left hand, *she* did hould,
      Who when *Muses poeticall she* sawe,
30   Unto my bed to be approached neare,
      Indittinge sonnets wch my woes might showe,
      W^th eies like fire inflamed, thus *she* spake. /
      P. These *harlotts Scænicall*° who doth permit,

─────────────────

      ² nether] neith[er] *MS*

Neare to this pensive patient to p[re]sume,
35   From helpinge these his paines who are so farre,
That they wth sugred poyson feed³ his greife.
ffor these are such, as wth unfruitfull weeds
Of passions, slay the graine of *reason* sound,
And do mans paines augment, not ease procure. /
40   Yf now some *Pesant base*, yo[ur] suttle baits
(As often tymes they do) should thus seduce,
I would not waighe so much, for them: for why?
In such my labour is not blemished;
But him you hurt, who hath ben trayned upp
45   In *Athens* studies *Academicall*.
Hence *Syrens* to destruction deepe depart,
Let *Muses mine*, attempt to cure his smart.
B. Thus they rebuked cast their face to ground,
And wth a *shamefast* blush they vanished.
50   But I, whose eies wth tricklinge teares were dim[m]e,
What woman *she*, of such imperious power
Might be, could not conceive, but daunted was,
And to the earth my countenance downe cast,
I marked what *she* would attempt at last.
55   Then nearer *she* beginninge to approach,
Uppon the furthest corner of my bed
Sate downe, my face behoulding ernestly
W^ch wth my wayling playnts, was pensive made.
And groveling to the ground wth griping greife,
60   In verses following, mans passions sore,
             W^ch mated mynds oppresse, *she* did deplore. /

Meter · 2 · /   2 · [r]

How is mans mynd plunged, alas, in paines,
Made sensles blocke, forsaking reasons light,
To darknes deepe he doth let loose the reines,
When cloudes of cares increase by fatall might.
5   *This man, late free from fond⁴ affections chaines,*
The heavens motions did perceive aright,

---

³ feed] *letter over-written as* "d"
⁴ fond] "u" *deleted after* "o" *MS*

The blazinge beames of Phœbus beauty cleare,
Cold Phœbes nature did to him appeare. /

And wandring starres, that retrograde do goe,
10   By sundry motions chaunginge in the skye,
Throughe helpe of arte, he did attaine to know,
Searchinge the depth of nature to descry,
Whose secret causes he could soundly showe,
Althoughe concealed they profoundly ly,
15   Why blustring blasts, do tosse the toylinge tyde,
What spirit doth the rowling heavens guide.

Why twinckling starres, settinge in Ocean sea,
Do shortly rise againe in radiant East,
Who doth the spring in such a temper swaye,
20   That fertile earth, with fragrant flowers is drest,
Who doth Autumnus grapes so full conveye,
Now blind he lies, with fetters strong opprest,
        And since fond fantasies his senses bound,
        His eies he fixeth on the basest ground. /

Prose 2 ·

But tyme a salve, said *she*, not wayling seekes,
Her eies on me *she* fixing then thus spake.
Art thou not he, who nursed wth o[ur] breast,
Fedd wth o[ur] foode, to mans estate attain'd?[5]
5   Such furniture on thee we did bestow,
W^ch if thou hadst not careleslie reiected,
From maladie they now had thee protected.
Knowest thou not me? Why dost thou silence keepe?
Is it for shamefastnes, or sensles feare? /
10   I rather wish it modest bashfulnes:[6]
But I perceive astonishment is cause. /
And when not only still, but wanting use
Of tounge, *she* me beheld, *her* hand *she* lay'd
Softly uppon my[7] breast, and thus *she* sayd.

---

[5] attain'd?] "," *altered to* "?" *MS*
[6] bashfulnes] *written in dark ink*
[7] my] head *deleted after* my *MS*

15   Here is no perill, into *lethargie*,
      This man is fallen, to deluded mynds
      A com[m]on greife. Him self he hath forgot,
      W^{ch} he againe to mynde will quickly call,
      When me more perfectly he shall perceive,
20   W^{ch} y^t he may performe, let us prepare
      His dim[m]ed eies to cleare from clouds of care. /
          This said, myne eies flowing wth floudes of teares,
          Wth foulded garment wypinge dry, *she* cleares. /   [2 v]

                        Meter 3[8]
      Night then expeld, me glomy darknes left,
      And former sight returned to mine eyes,
      Like as the sunne, of wonted light bereft,
      When blustringe blasts, of whirling wyndes aryse. /
5   *When hidden Pole with clustred clouds doth stand,*
      Starres dimmed not displaied in skowlinge skye,
      Nights misty darknes, spred on lowringe° land,
      Which when as boystrous Boreas mightely
      Retiringe from the hollow Thrasian den,
10   *Shall from the skies expell restoring day:*
      Faire Phœbus former light doth shine againe,
      Whose radiant beames mans dazeled eyes dismay. /

                        Prose 3 · /
      No otherwise the vapo[urs] of my greife
      Expelled claine, my mynd acknowledged
      The countennance of my *Phisitian.*
      Wherefore when I on *her* myne eies had fixt,
5   My *Nurse Philosophie* I plaine perceiv'd,
      In whose lappe lulled longe I did converse.
      Are you, quoth I, Mistress[9] of vertues all,
      To desarts of *exile* descended lowe,
      From highe? Would you wth me a porc[i]on take
10   Wth forged crymes accused? Then *she* spake.
      P. Should I thee leave my sonne, and not beare[10] part

---

[8] *Meter 3*] *Meter 2 MS*
[9] Mistress] M^{rs} *MS*
[10] beare] "e" *inserted above with caret after* "b"

Of this thy burden wch thou dost sustaine
Because thie enimies do thee envy?
And thee most in[n]ocent, alone to bare /
15   For *dame Philosophie* unfit it were,
Should I mans blamings feare? Or staggring stand
As if some strange successe to thee befell?
Hast thou not noted how in every age,
Wise men are vexed by the wickeds rage?
20   Wth follies furies before *Plato* lived
Have not we strugled sore? And in his daies
His maister *Socrates* (I standing by)
Of death iniurious gained victory,
Whose large inheritaunce of knowledge sound,
25   *Lewd Epicures, Stoickes,* and other sects,
Like spoiles in warr, against my will did snatch /
My garments, wch my hands had made, who rent,
And every sect therefrom purloin'd a patch,
Supposing so they should me wholely catch.
30   And thus wth prey[11] these *Pyrates* did depart,
In whom, because some remants of attire
W^{ch} I had worne, appeared, folly rash   3 ·/[r]
My freinds familiar esteeming them,
Wth com[m]on *Error* did seduce the most. /
35   But if exile of *Anaxagoras,*
Nor *Socrates* his poyson thou dost knowe,
Nor *Zeno* wth his tortures being strange,
Yet *Canius* freinds and wrongs of *Seneca,*
Also *Soranus* freinds[12] whose fame not old
40   Nor unrenowned flies, thou mightest marke.
Of all whose wrongs, the only reason was,
Because, in wisdoms p[re]cepts trayn'd by mee,
From wicked men theire mynds did disagree.
Wherfore so to admire no cause thou hast
45   Yf wee, in such a surginge sea of life,
Wth toylinge tempests strugling sore, be tost:
Sith wee against all vice, o[ur] power oppose,

---

[11] prey] pray *MS*
[12] and wrongs of *Seneca,* / Also *Soranus* freinds] *inserted above with caret after Canius*
freinds

Whose army thoughe it infinite appeare,
Yet wicked wretches troupes wee neede not feare. /
50   For why? Wthout all regiment they march
To rash attempts, inconstant here and there,
Blind *Error* only doth theire forces leade.
Who, when against us they do most p[re]vaile,
Our Prince to turret stronge her *goodes* wthdrawes. /
55   Unfruitfull stuffe to gaine they only strive,
But wee, from furious tumults, most secure,
        Stronge fenced, where fooles rage cannot aspire,
        Deride such doltes, who basest trash require. /

                        Meter 4 · /
Who so syncerely doth, in setled state,
Treade under foote proud fortunes ficle fate:
In chances[13] change who constant can endure,
Unchanginge countenance conservinge pure:
5   *No swelling seas from bottome billowes turninge,*
Nor mount Vesevus flashing flames feirce burninge,
No thunderbolts (though turrets peirce they can)
May much amaze the mynd of such a man.
Why do men wretched so much Tyrants feare?
10   *Or them admire, whose rage doth weake appeare?*
Hope thou for nothinge, dread no enemy,
And thou unarmest ire of tyrannye. /
But who so tremblinge feares, or hopes at all,
(Because his will included is in thrall)
15   *Reiecteth reasons sheild, and sound security,*
His mynd imprisoninge in instability. /   3 [v]

                        Pro: 4 · /
Dost thou, quoth *shee*, these things not understand?
And are they not imprinted in thy mynd?
Art thou like blockish *Asse* before the harpe?
Why weapest thou? Why dost thou flowe in teares?
5   Declare thy greife, nothing from me conceale.
If thou *Phisitians* helping hand expect,
It's requisit thy wound be first displayed.

---

[13] *chances] second "c" altered from "g"*

Bo: Then I recalling strength of mynd, thus said[:] /
Doth yet a further declaration neede?

10 Doth *fortunes furie* not yet full appeare?
Doth sight of prison base you nothing move?
Is this the *librarie*, wthin my howse
As certaine Mansion place, wch you did chose?
Wherin of mortall, and divine affaires

15 Sitting wth me, you often would discourse?
Had I this habit and this pensive hewe,
When *Natures* secrets I did search wth you?
When you starres motions manifest did make,[14]
When manners o[urs], and all o[ur] course of life,

20 Like *heavens order* firme to frame, you taught.
Is this the guerdon° wch wee only gaine,
Who strive yo[ur] p[re]cepts strictlie to observe?
By *Plato* you this sentence ratified,
Where wise men rule, such kingdoms happie are,

25 Or where to wisdome, kinges addict ther care.
By him also you have admonished,
That for iust cause wise men should take the rule,
Lest raines of Realme *bad men* to them transport,
Wherby they may oppresse the better sort.

30 This grave advice wch I by you was taught
In study privat, into publick act
Of regiment I wished to reduce. /
You and y^t *God* wch unto learned mynds
Infuseth wisdomes *Arts*, are witnesses,

35 Y^t nothing save the com[m]on good of all
To Magistracie did my mynd perswade,
Hence wth bad men I waged still debate,
And this my conscience hath freely cleared,
In rights defense no mans offence I feared. /

40 How often violence, and pore mens wronges,
By *Conigastus* offred, did I crosse?
How oft *Triguilla great* in *Palace* swaying
In wrongs nere finished did I resist?
How oft poore wreches vexed wofully

45 By lawles lucre° of the *Barbarous*, 4 [r]

---

[14] make] "r" *deleted after* "a" *MS*

Wth hazard of my state did I maintaine?
From right to wrong no man could me reclaime. /
Hard haps of *Provinces* I did bewayle,
No less then they themselves to see them sacked
50   Wth private spoils, and publicke tribute racked.
In tyme of famine when exac[i]on sore
Wth penury did pinch *Campania*,
I undertooke (yea though the *Kinge* perceived)
For com[m]on good 'gainst officer to strive,
55   And y^t such prowlinge[15] ceast I did procuer.
Noble *Paulline*, whose substance *Palace dogs*
By gredy gaine and pride sought to devoure,
Out of their rav[en]inge iawes I rescued. /
Envious *Cyprian*, who to condemne
60   *Albinus Consulate* uniustlie sought,
Before his cause was tryd I did wthstand.
Did not I kindle *Envies* flame herein?
Yet (thoughe in Court, for *Iustice* sake disgraced),[16]
I ought of oth[ers] to have been embraced. /
65   But how base men my iustest cause defaced! /
Basill from *Kinges* affaires long since expell'd,
Me to accuse wth bribes suborned° was,
Wheras *Opilio*, and *Gaudentius*,
For wrongs and treacheries most villanous,
70   By censure of the *Kinge* to be exiled
Condemned were, when they in *Sanctuary*
Would shroud themselves, and not the *Kinge* obey,
It being tould the *Kinge*, he did proclaime,
Unles *Ravenna* they would shortlie leave,
75   Wth markes in forehead burned they should packe.° /
What more severe then sentence such may seeme?
But they that verie day accusing mee,
Their slanders were of great authoritie.
Why? Have my sundry studies this deserv'd?
80   Is not this shame if not y^t innocent
I am condemned? Accusers basenes might
Make *fortune* blush to see me thus abused?

---

[15] prowlinge] powlinge *MS (translating Latin coemptio)*
[16] disgraced),] disgraced,) *MS*

Now marke the crimes wherof I am accused.
They did obiect y^t senators I saved.
85   And how? They urge that I informers staied,
Who brought intelligence that guiltie found
The whole *Senat* of treason to the crowne.
What then I answered (*o Lady*) iudge. /
The fact I did denie. For should I rushe
90   To such attempts as would force you to blush?   [4 v]
Yet I confesse, I would, and ever will
Endeavour to assist the *Senators*,
But will not seek intelligence to stay. /
Is y^t offence to save their state to wish?
95   The *Senats* sentence made it great offence,
But ignorance of things too credulous,
Fore past deserts cannot againe recall. /
Neither did *Socrates* esteeme it fitt,
For to conceale a truth, or grant a lye.
100   Iudge you, and let the wise discusse these things,
The course and truth wherof to memory,
Wth penne I leave to all posteritie.
What should I now in vaine make menc[i]on
Of letters falsly forged and imposed,
105   Whereby the *Romaine* freedome to restore
I should attempt, untruly they obiect?
Whose treacheries had ben made manifest,
If to accusers, (wch in causes greate
Hath no small force), I might have had accesse.
110   What hope[17] of libertie can now remaine?
Would *God* some hope[18] were left. Wth *Canius* words
I answer would, who when he was accus'd
By *Caius Cæsar* sonne of *Germanicke*,
Of secret treason wrought against his *Throne*,
115   Thus said: If I had knowne, thou hadst not knowne. /
I waile not thus to see bad men conspire
Vertue to vexe, but how vile practizes
They can effect I greatlie do admire.
Perhapps my weakenes worser things would wish.

---

[17] hope] "o" *deleted after* "o" *MS*
[18] hope] "o" *deleted after* "o" *MS*

120   But wicked men against the in[n]ocent
          At plesure theirs for to accomplish wrong
          Before *Gods* presence, doth seem monstrous strange. /
          Hence one of yo[ur] *Philosophers* and freinds,
          And not w[th]out iust cause demanded thus. /
125   *Howe com[m]eth evill, if their be a God?*
          If their be not a God, how cometh good?
          But now allthoughe such blind bloudthirstie myndes,
          Who practize all good men to undermyne
          My ruine sought, because I did protect
130   Good men, ye all the *Senators*, did I
          No greater favour at those fathers hands
          Whose lives from death I saved, then deserve?
          You (*Lady deare*) remember well I thinke
          Who use my words and deeds still to direct. /
135   You know, I say, that in *Verona*[19] townc,
          When *Theodoricus* most blouddy *Kinge*   5 ·/[r]
          Suspected treason laid to *Albins* chardge
          Unto the whole *Senate* sought to translate:
          W[th] what greate danger I did them defend.
140   You knowe the truth I speake, not wont to boast.
          ffor hauty harts deserve noe praise but blame,
          Who bragginge hunt to reape reward of fame.
          But what event myne in[n]ocency got,
          You see, insteade of vertues iust reward
145   Of vilest vice reproche I do sustaine. /
          Could mans confession of a guiltie fact,
          Iudges so to consent severely cause,
          As neith[er] *Error* of mans iudgment fraile,
          Nor *fortunes* ficklenes unstaid to all
150   Might any one of them move to remorse?
          If *sacred churches*, I had ben accused
          To set on fire. Yf w[th] bloud sucking sword
          To murther *Preistes*. Yf *good men* to subvert
          Yet sentence peremptory ought not[20] passe,
155   Till I my fact confesse, and p[re]sent be,

---

[19] *Verona*] "r" *deleted after* "r" *MS*
[20] not] to *deleted after* not *MS*

Or ells convicted were by laws decree. /
But I then distant allmost fiftie miles,
None ther to plead my cause, for my good will
Unto the *Senat* shew'd, by *Senatours*
160 To death, and poore proscription am condemn'd. /
O blessed, whom such crime cannot convince,
Whose *dignity* th'accusers also sawe,
W^{ch} that wth cursed crymes they might obscure
They forged y^t I, for promoc[i]on
165 Wth *Negromancy* did my soule pollute. /
But you in mee desier of mortall dregs
Have cleansed cleane, unlawful in yo[ur] sight
Was *sacrilege*. For in my eares, and mynd,
Pythagoras his speech you did inspire.
170 *One God, not many Gods, wee ought to serve,*
Base *Devils* ayde for me would seeme unfit,
Whom you in state procuer, like *God* to sitt. /
Besids my vertuous wife, and honest freinds,
And reverend *father* worthy *Symmachus,*
175 Suspition of such cryme from me remove.
O wicked fact, sustaine I do such blame,
Because wth you, in study sole I live,
And sith wth p[re]cepts yo[urs] I am adorn'd,
Like such I seeme as deale wth *Spirits vile.* /
180 Thus unto mee yo[ur] dignitie in vaine
Is both estem'd, and you like wronge sustaine /   [5 v]
To these are added further heaps of harme,
Deserts in things, light iudgment of most men
Regardeth not but *fortunes* false event.
185 They iudge prosperitie *God* only guides,
Hence, good report afflicted wretches loose.
What rumo[urs] strange, and speches dissonant
On mee are made, I greive to call to mynd.
Of miseries this sorest burden is,
190 When one of crimes accused is, thoughe pure,
Men iudge they well deserve what they endure.
And I alas, from all my goods exil'd,
Deprived of renowne, in name defyl'd,
For benefits, this punishment sustaine.
195 Me thinks I now behould despitefull flocks

Of mynds envious, clapping hands for ioye. /
The cursed crue, new coyning crimes uniust,
Good men, by terror of my toyles dismay'd,
Bad men, because they see no punishment,
200   Foule facts to undertake emboldened,
And to performe vice, moved by rewards,
    And guiltles men voyd of security,
    W^{th}out defense. Wherefore thus may we cry.

Meter 5

O thou creator of the starry sky,
Triumphinge in eternall throne, whose might
Swift heavens motion guideth orderly,
Ordaininge Planets for to march aright.
5   *So that sometyme full Moone shineth cleare,*
            In opposition to her brother faire,
            Smale starres from humaine sight
            Who doth detaine,
            And neare his beames, her light
10   *She wants againe. /*

And Hesperus appearinge over night,
Behind the Sonne the frostie starres to leade,
Is named Lucifer, in morninge bright
Before the light of Phœbus beemes convaide.
15   *In winter shorter dayes thy wisdome made,*
            When fallinge leaves by nippinge frost do fade.
            Againe in Sommer tyde,
                Thy divine powers,
            Most equally devide,
20   *Nights swifter houres. /*   6 · [r]

Thy might doth moderate chaunginge yeare,
So as greene leaves late flourishinge in springe,
Which winters boystrous blasts from trees doth teare,
Succedinge seasons calme againe will bringe. /
25   *And that in Vernall tyme what seedes men sowe,*
            Doth scorchinge Syrius cause full ripe to growe.
            Yea nothing lucid free
            From former state,

Forsaketh the decre
30   *Made firme by fate.*

All thinges thou dost dispose to certaine end
Actions of men only thou dost reiect
O governour to mortall men descend
Do not our miserable cause neglect.
35   *For why doth fortune fraile such courses chaunge?*
Men guiltlesse are condemn'd to torments strange,
Whose punishments were fitt
For men impure:
But wicked wretches sitt
40   *In seates secure. /*

Whose pride treades downe, by course of fate uniust,
The sacred neckes of reverend Saints most rare,
Vertue contemned is to corners thrust,[21]
Of cursed crymes Iust men condemned are.
45   *No periury, no fraude at all anoyeth:*
Nor forged falshood vicious men destroyeth.
But Kinges they can subdue
At hartes desire,
Maugre° their Subiects[22] *true*[23]
50   *Who*[24] *them admyre. /*

O now at last respect wretched mankind,
Thou, who contrivinge heavens fixed frame,
Events of all thinges els dost firmely binde,
Of all thy workes men are not least of name
55   *Yet tossed still we toyle in fortunes sea.*
Whose walowinge waves (o moderator) swaye. /
And in what constant state
Heaven remayneth:
Confirme our ficle fate,
60   *Whom earth contayneth. /*

---

[21] thrust] thurst *MS*
[22] *Subiects*] "e" *inserted above with caret*
[23] true] crue *MS*
[24] who] "m" *deleted after* "o" *MS*

Pro: 5 /

When thus I howlinge still my woes bewrayd,°
Not moved wth my plaints *she* smyling sayd.
When first thee sad and sobbing sore I saw   [6 v]
By miseries and banishment thy state
5   Opprest to stand, I streight imagined. /
But yet, unles thy speach had thee betrayd,
Thy cheife exile was not by me bewrayd.° /
From *Natures* soile thou art not farre expeld,
But thence dost straye. If needs thou wilt maintaine
10   Y^t thou expulsed art, then blame thy selfe. /
For non but thou thy self, could thee exile.
Yf thou thy *native soyle* to mynd recall,
It is not ruled by the multitude
Like *Athens* wonted *Popular estate,*
15   But here *one Kinge, one Prince* directeth all
In many *Cittizens* who doth delight,
Inhabitants not seeking to expell.
Whose lawes decree, whose iustice to obey
Is cheifest liberty. That auntient lawe
20   In *reasons Citty* made, dost thou not knowe?
Prohibitinge such subiects banishment,
W^thin her wales who fix their mansion place?
In whose p[re]cinct environed who stands,
No doubt he never doth *exile* deserve. /
25   But who so wisheth from her seate to stray,
He ceaseth to deserve therin to stay. /
Wherefore to find thee in this desert place,
So much I weighe not as thy chaunged mynd. /
Adorned *Ivory* wales wth pearles of price
30   In wonted *librarye* appearing late,
So much I seek not, as thy seate of mynd:
Wherin not bookes, but y^t wch bookes doe grace,
Profoundest *sentences* I late did place. /
Touching thy care for others *common good,*
35   A true relac[i]on thou has published.
Yet in respect of ample merits thine,
Only some part of thy deserts dost touch.
Concerning crymes obiected unto thee
Had they been truly prov'd they honest were. /

40 And part therof were false surmises forged,
      As thou hast unto all made manifest.
      Concerning thine accusers crimes and fraudes
      Breiflie the truth thou hast deciphered. /
      For fame still prying into all mens acts
45 More copiouslie will celebrate such facts.
      Against the *Senats* sentence rigorous
      Thou hast wth vehemence inveyed well.
      My defamac[i]on, and thine owne disgrace   7 [r]
      Thou hast[25] aright bewayled. / Finally
50 Thy gripinge greife did growe to galeing ire
      Against *dame fortune*, playninge y^t rewards
      To *good and evil men* unequall happe.[26]
      Endinge thy raginge sonnet wth request
      Y^t earth, like heavens constant state, might rest.
55 But sith trumoylinge passions tumult reigne
      Greif, *Ire*, and anguish thee distractinge sore:
      Stronger receipts (as now thy state doth stand)
      I may not yet apply. I first must use
      More easie helps a while, that this desease
60 Puft up wth perturbac[i]ons pinchinge paines,
            And swellinge sore, may first be mollified:
            That stronger meanes may after be applied. /

                              Meter · 6 ·
      With Phœbus blasinge beames when Cancer boyles,
      In earth untymely who so sewes his seede:
      Deceaved much of Ceres fruits to speede,
      May acornes eate, for all his frustrate toyles. /

5   *With winters windes when you see naked feildes,*
      Walke not the woodes to finde the violet:
      Nor fragrant flowers wth gredy hand to get.
      Yf grapes you gather would, such Autume yeildes. /

      Eternall God ordayneth seasons all,
10 *Guidinge their actions not by fortune mixed,*

---

[25] hast] w^th *deleted after* hast *MS*
[26] happe] "n" *deleted after* "e" *MS*

Not *changinge courses* w^(ch) *his wisdome fixed,*
So *what this order rashly leaves shall fall.*

Prose 6 · /
First then wilt thou w^(th) patience me abide,
W^(th) questions fewe to search and to decyde
Thy state of mynd, y^(t) I may understand,
The meanes thy sore to salve. *Bo: Lady* demand
5   What seemeth good, I will my²⁷ mynd disclose. /
Ph: Dost thou by rash and headlonge chaunce suppose
This world is toßed? Or dost thou assure
Thy selfe, ther is a rule of reason pure?
Bo: Things certaine in uncertaine course to goe
10   I never can beleive. But *God* I know
The world doth guide, w^(ch) he in wisdome made,   [7 v]
From truth wherof no age can me diswade. /
Ph: Tis true, quoth *shee,* in verse thou songe this late. /
Only mankind to be exempt of fate
15   And divine providence, thou didst lament:
All els to stand by reasons regiment
Thou doubted not, wherfore I marvaile much
Havinge y^(t) iudgment sound, thy greife is such. /
But let us deeper search thy deepth of wound,
20   Some causes hid thy mated thoughts confound.
But tell me, sith by *God* world firm to 'byde
Thou doubtest not, by what meanes doth he guide?
Bo: This questions meaning full I scarse conceive,
Wherfore unanswered the same I leave. /
25   *Ph:* Did I not truly iudge, then answered *shee,*
Imagininge some other want to be:
Wherby like gredy *Gulphe* into thy mynd
Deseases crept of perturbac[i]ons blind. /
But dost thou knowe of things what is the end,
30   Or where to *natures* actions cheiflie tend?
Bo: I have this hard: Now sighing sorrowes vaine
My memory obscured much detaine. /
Ph: But dost thou knowe from whence all things proceede?
Bo: I say from *God. P:* How can this *error* breede,

---

²⁷ my] *inserted above with caret*

35   Y^t wheras the begining thou dost knowe
      Of things, what is the end thou canst not show?
      But such are passions pollicies and power,
      Mans reason they will shake, yea quite devo[ur],
      But wholly it to quench they never can. /
40   But answere yet: knowest thou, thou art a man?
      B: I doubt not y^t. P: What is man then declare?
      B: This trifle do you aske?[28] I know men are
      Made reasonable creatures and mortall,
      This I do know and nothing doubt at all. /
45   And this my self to be I do confesse.
      Ph: And nothinge more? B: Nothing: P: Now I do gesse
      Anoth[er] greatest cause of this thy smart,
      Thou ceasest to remember what thou art.
      The causes of thy care I see full sure,
50   And find a meanes wherby I may thee[29] cure.
      For now because thy selfe to knowe thou failest,
      Exile and losse of goodes thou thus bewaylest.
      Because thou dost not knowe the finall end   8 [r]
      Of things, to wicked men thou dost contend
55   Strength and felicity for to abide,
      Because by what meanes *God* the world doth guide
      Thou hast forgot, thou iudgest courses change
      Wthout a guide, by *fortunes* motions strange. /
      These causes are, not causinge greife alone
60   But these procure certaine destruction.
      But, to the Author of all health be praise,
      For in thee wholely *nature* not decayes.
      Greate meanes wee have diseases to p[re]vent,
      In y^t thou touchinge Creatures regiment
65   A truth dost hould, y^t *fortunes* ficlenes
      Doth not beare rule, but *God* wth stablenes. /
      Doubt not therof from this smale sparke of thine
      Shall vitall heate revivinge shortlie shine. /
      But in as much as for these maladies
70   Time doth not yet require stronge remydies:
      And this is naturall, when sentence true

---

[28] aske?] "," *deleted after* "e" *with* "?" *inserted above*
[29] thee] the *MS*

From mynds reiected is, *errors* ensue:
Wherby affections mists, mens sights obscure.
I first by gentil meanes will this procure,
75   To mittigate thy paine, that passions blind
     Expelled cleane: truthes brightnes thou maist finde. /

[Meter 7]

Starres cannot yeild their wonted light
When they by cloudes be hid from eye. /
If surginge Sea by sturdy spite[30]
Of whirlinge windes unquiet ly,
5   *Though late his billowes were as bright*
As clearest day in christall sky,
Man may not peirce them wyth his sight,
In that they muddy are thereby. /
The river swift runinge aright
10   *From craggie top of mountaines high,*
If loosed rockes slide downe with might,
The stopped streame will runne awrye. /
If thou likewise (o mortall wight)
Require truth clearly to descrie,°
15   *In reasons path if thou delight*
Ioy, Feare, Hope, Greife, repell and fly.
     Thy mynd obscure, like misty night,
     Wher these do raigne, fond fancies tye. /

$ [31]

---

³⁰ *spite*] *spit MS*
³¹ $] *final flourish ending Book I (a unique decoration in MS)*

THE · PHYSICKE · OF · PHILOSOPHY ·
compiled by Anicius Manlius Torquatus
Severinus Boethius touchinge
the consolation of Lady
Philosphy in the
tyme of his
exile ·

The second booke expressing the
preparative before she applieth stronger receipts ·

The first Prose[1] *· /*
This said a while *she* paus'd. And when *she* sawe
By silence still my mynds attention
She thus began. *P.* Yf fully I conceive
The causes and the habit of thy greife,
5   For ardent love of former fortune lost
Thou languishest. / *She* beinge changed sole,
Thy state of mynd doth change, as thou dost iudge.
I know this monsters manyfould deceipts,
So longe wth them, whom *she* meanes to delude,
10   *She* fawninge freindship shewes, till *she* confound
Wth galeinge greife, whom *shee* in deepe despaire
Dismisseth drown'd. / Whose *nature*, use, desert,
If thou to mynd recall, no worthy thinge
By her thou didst enioye, or ells hast lost
15   Whatever worthy was, thou shalt perceive.
But these things to thy mynd much to revoke
I need not, for thou usedst to invay
Wth vehemence against her, when at hand

---

[1] *Prose]* "P" *written over erasure*

Fawninge wth thee *shee* was in smiling wise,
20   Wth sentences suggested from my selfe.
But suddaine change of *state* doth seldome chance
Wthout a certaine conflict first of mynd.
So thou art somewhat from mynds rest declin'd. /
But tyme requires y^t thou shouldst now receive
25   And tast some soft and pleasant sweet receipt,
W^{ch} inward taken may p[re]pare the way
For phisicke forcyble. Wherfore swete voyce
Of *Rethoricke* draw neare, wch then aright
Proceeds, when p[re]cepts myne *she* doth not passe. /
30   And when like *musickes note shee* seemes to change,
Sometymes ascending highe, somtymes more base,   9 [r]
What is it then (*o man*) wch thee hath cast
Into this agonie? I iudge some change
Thou hast beheld, unusuall, and strange. /
35   If thou supposest *fortune* changed is,
Thy selfe thou dost deceive. / These allwaies are
Her manners, this her nature is. / To thee
She rath[er] constancy in change doth showe.
No other wise *she* was, when *she* wth bayts
40   Of counterfeit felicity on thee
Did fawne. / Of *goddes* blind the ficle face
Thou hast descri'd,° wch yet from oth[er] men
Concealed hath it selfe, to thee made knowne. /
Yf *she* content thee, use her wthout plainte,
45   Her ficlenes pernitious if thou fear'st
Contemne, reiect, her daliance dangerous.
For y^t wch caused hath thee to lament,
Ought to have been the cause of thy content.
She hath thee left, whom who so will not leave,
50   Secure shall never live. Dost thou esteeme
Y^t happines, wch is not permanent?
Is *fortune* deare to thee, who neither doth
Constant abide, and when *she* doth depart
Behind *her* leaveth waylinge wofullnes?
55   Yf neith[er] sure *she* can contayned be,
And when *she* doth depart, leaves misery:
What els is fading *fortune* but a note
Of future miserie? Neith[er] suffice

It doth things set before o[ur] eies, to veiwe.
60   But wisdome constant things event doth prove,
Who feares not *fortunes* frownes, nor seekes her love.
Lastlie wth constant mynd abide content
Thou must, what so is done in *fortunes* rule.
Under *her yoake* sith thou dost stand subdu'd.
65   But if to *her a lawe* thou wilt p[re]scribe,
Whom willinglie thy *mistris* thou hast made:
Commanding *her* to stay or to depart:
Were not y^t wronge? And by *impatience*
Thou dost augment thy *state* of misery,
70   W^ch is not altered at all thereby.
Yf to the winds thy sailes thou dost com[m]it
Thou dost not saile whither thy will would wish
But whith[er] winds will drive. Yf to the ground
Thy seede thou dost commit, dost thou command
75   Fruitfull and barren yeares? To *fortunes* rule
Thy selfe thou yeilded hast, thy *Mistris will*
Thou must obey, yet thou *her* whirlinge wheele
        To stop dost strive, most simple sott thou art,
        Yf *fortune* stand, *her nature* would depart.   [9 v]

Meter 1 · /

When she in pride her course intendes to change,
Like swellinge tyde, wch raginge like doth range:
She treades downe Kinges, who dreadfull were of late,
And honour bringes to them of base estate.
5   *She hardlie heares the wretched poore mens cryes,*
Nor cares for teares of wofull wepinge eies.
She small doth passe for sighinge sobs of greife,
Wherof she was her selfe the Agent cheife. /
She dalieth so, she practizeth her power,
10   *And men doth showe monstrouse events each houre.*
Now may you see a man in wealth abounde,
Whom shortly she intendeth to confounde.[2]

---

[2] confounde] "u" *deleted after first* "o" *MS*

Prose · 2 · /

But now³ wᵗʰ thee, in *fortunes* person, I
Would argue thus. Wherfore observe this well,
Yf lawe may not this thinge of thee requier. /
Why dost thou thus (*o man*) wᵗʰ plaints me vexe,

5   Me guilty pleadinge still? What iniury
Have I thee done? What *goodes* of thine have I?
Concerning right of wealth and dignities
Wᵗʰ mee contend, let who so will be⁴ iudge,
And if to any man these do thou provest,

10   I frely grant those thine, wᶜʰ thou requirest. /
When *nature naked* from thy mothers wombe
Brought thee forth wantting all things, I thee tooke,
Wᵗʰ my *goodes* thee sustained, and why then
Art thou wᵗʰ me impatient? Wᵗʰ love

15   In carefull sort I have the cherished
And wᵗʰ abundance, and wᵗʰ ornaments
Of all my proper goods I have the deckt.
My hand now to wᵗʰdrawe it is my will,
Thanke me for yᵗ my *goodes* thou hast enioyd

20   So long, no cause thus to complaine thou hast
As if thou wert deprived of thy owne.
Why dost thou sigh thefore? I have no wronge
Unto thee done! *Riches and honours highe*
And all such like to mee by right pertaine.

25   Like handmaydes these, there *lady* me account.
Wᵗʰ mee they come, if I goe, they depart.
Bouldly I dare affirm, if these were thine
Whose want thou waylest, them thou hadst not lost. /
Shall I alone my lawfull right to use

30   Controwled be? Tis lawfull for the *skyes*
Sometyme cleare daies, sometymes darke nights to cause. /
Tis lawfull for the yeare, the face of earth
Wᵗʰ flowers and fruit, or stormes and cold to change. /
Tis lawfull for the *Sea* a calme to cause,   10 ·[r]

35   Sometyme to rage and swell wᵗʰ waves and stormes. /

---

³ now] the *deleted after* now *MS*
⁴ will be] wilbe *MS*

Shall malecontented mynd of man, my waies
Alone to constant courses still constraine?
This is my power, this sport I exercise
My whirlinge whele full fast about I turn.
40   Things lowe wth highe, and highe wth low I match. /
Ascend at pleasure thine, yet if my play
Bid thee discend, disdain not to obey. /
My wonted use hast thou not understood?
Hast thou not knowne that *Crœsus Lydian Kinge*
45   Whom *Cyrus* feared much not longe before,
Captive became to him wthin a while,
Who cast into the flaminge fire to dy
Safe from the same by storm from *sky* did scape? /
Pallus hast thou forgot? Whom pittie moved
50   Wth trickling teares, the woes of *Persian Kinge*
Captive to him subdued, to lament?
What els do cryes of tragedies bewayle,
But y^t *dame fortune Kingdomes* doth⁵ subverte?
In *Athens* yong hast thou not learned late,
55   That in *Ioves porch of wine two vessels ly,*
Wherof the one is *good*, the oth[er] *bad.*
What if of *good* more store, thou hast enioyed?
What if from thee I wholely am not fledd?
What if this change iust cause, for thee to hope
60   For future happines in tyme procure?
Yet howsoever, let thy mynd be firme.
    And sith thou art in common state of life,
    Wth all mankind, cease this unlawfull strife. /

[Meter 2]

If Lady Abaundance should open her dore,
Vouchsafinge to man much gould and riches store:
Heapinge as Sea doth sand, discharge uppon the land,
Or thicke as starres do stand,
5   *Men weepe for more. /*

Though God in benignity no good denieth,
But wealth and dignity franckly applieth:

---

⁵ doth] th *inserted above with caret after* "o"

For all such favour greate, it semeth nothinge yet,
But gapinge still to get

10
                                      for more he cryeth. /

What reason can lymits set to such desire,
When thirstines more to gett burnes as a fire?
Though man in wealth abound, such have not riches found,
Whom waylinge want doth wounde

15
                                      More to require. / [10 v]

                    Pro: 3 ·
If thus should *fortune* in lawe wth thee pleade
No cause to contradict her could you showe. /
But if by right you can yo[ur] cause^6 confirme
Spare not to speake I freely give you leave. /
5   *Bo*: These reasons verilie are singuler,
Wth *Rethoricke* and *Musicke* sauced sweete.
So longe as they are hard they do delight,
But sharper sence of harmes men wretched have. /
Wherfore noe soner you had ceast to speeke,
10   But gripinge greife my hart began to breake. /
Ph: A truth it is. These are not cures of greife,
But light p[re]paretives more fitt for cure
Thy *maladie* to make. For stronge receipts
W^{ch} deeper peirce, hereafter I will use.
15   But lest thie selfe in wofull state thou iudge
The manifould and worthy happines
W^{ch} thou dost still enioye, hast thou forgott?
I cease to shewe the care of cheifest men
To thee an *Orphan* shew'd, elected fitt
20   To marry in the race of *Princes* cheife,
And y^t wch in nere freindshipp doth excell
Beloved first, then maryed you were.
Who will not thee most fortunate account?
When as they shall consider the *Renowne*
25   And *honour* of the father of thy wife,
And shall respect thy vertuous wife, and sonnes.
I here omitt (for common *goodes* I passe)

---

^{6} cause] cause *deleted after* cause MS

The *honours* of thy youth on thee bestowed,
W^{ch} many older men deserved not.
30 Thy *heape of happines* I only touch,
Yf any part of happines remaine,
In mortall state, may then the memory
Of thy renowne by any heapes of harmes,
Be blotted out of mynd? Where as thou hast
35 Thy sonnes both⁷ *Consuls* at one tyme beheld,
Attended on by many *Senators*,
Brought from theire howse wth multitudes applause.
When they in court on iudgmente seate were set
Thou beinge chosen *Orator* didst win[n]e
40 Of wit and flowinge eloquence the fame. /
When thou betwen the *Consuls* both thy sonnes
The expectac[i]on of the standers by
With loftie speach didst fully satisfie.
Dame fortune thou I think deceived hast
45 While thee her cheife delight *she* hath extoll'd⁸
Such gift as never unto private man
She would impart, from *her* thou taken hast.
Wilt thou with fortune therfore cast account?
With lowringe° loke now first on thee *shee* frownes
50 Yf thou of ioies, and of thy fate adverse   11 [r]
The nu[m]ber and the manner dost observe:
Thy state as yet happie thou must confesse. /
But if thy state thou deem'st unfortunate,
Because thy seminge⁹ ioyes are banished:
55 Yet maist thou not be thought in wretched state,
Because thy seming greifes are vanished. /
Dost thou uppon the stage of mortal fate
Now first on suddaine stranger like ascend?
What constancie doth rest in humaine state?
60 Sith unto man *death* will procure an end. /
Thoughe *fortune* chaunce to stay, yet *death* is *death*
Of *fortune* left thee. What odes canst thou make

---

⁷ both] "o" *deleted after* "o" *MS*
⁸ extoll'd] extolld *MS*
⁹ seminge] *word deleted after* seminge *MS*

Then wheth[er][10] thou by yeildinge upp thy breath
Leave her, or *she* by flyeinge, thee forsake? /

Meter 3 · /

When Phœbus bright
His beames begins to showe,
In charet cleare,
Starres at his light
5 *Obscurred darke doe growe*
And pale appeare.

When trees in springe
While Zephyr milde doth raigne
Are deckt with flowres:
10 *Stormes shortly bringe*
Them to decline againe
By winters showres. /

Oft tymes wee find
A calme on surginge sease
15 *And storme doth cease,*
Oft Boreas wind
Againe doth tempest rayse
Without release. /

20 *If mortall state*
Doth so abide unsure,
Then no state trust:
Nothinge by fate
Can constant longe endure,
25 *But change it must. /*

Prose · 4 ·

Bo: A true relac[i]on (*Nurse* of vertues all)
Thou here hast made, neither the race most swift   [11 v]
Of former happines may I deny.
But this my mynd recaling much doth vexe:
5   For in the miseries of *fortunes* fate,

---

[10] wheth[er]] "h" *inserted above with caret after* "w"

To have been happie, is most wofull state.
Ph: But for as much as thou deceived art
To thine estate thou maist no fault impute.[11]
For if vaine name of fraile felicity
10   Forpassed late, doth thy unrest procure,
Consider then how many and how greate
Abundant blessings yet wth thee remaine. /
If then what thinge in *fortunes* treasure cheife
Thou hast enioy'd, by providence devine,
15   The same to thee p[re]served is untoucht.
Canst thou best giftes retayninge, yet complaine
Of thy *mishap*? In saffety *Symmachus*
Y^t worthie *gemme* the father of thy wife
As yet doth live, and y^t wch dearer ought
20   Of thee to be esteemed then thy life,
A man he is both wise and vertuous. /
Careles of his, but carefull for thy wronges.
Thy modest wife in saftie likewise lives, /
In shamefast chastitie who doth excell.
25   And y^t I breiflie may her gifts relate,
Her fathers vertues *she* doth imitate.
She lives I say *her life* esteeming nought,
ffor thee *she* only doth the same conserve. /
Wherein thy *happines* only declineth,
30   Wth teares and greife for want of thee, *she* pineth. /
Thy children *Senators* what should I touche?
In whom (as much as may appeare in youth
The *Image* of their *Auncestors* is seen. /
Sith then mans cheifest care is of his life
35   Oh happie thou if thou thie state dydst[12] knowe)
Who yet possessest these more deare then life. /
Cease then thy cares, *fortune* doth not much frowne. /
Nor sturdie stormes thy *ship* do much assaile.
For freinds like ancors fixed firme remaine,
40   Who p[re]sent comfort neither will refraine,

---

[11] impute] art *deleted with* ute *inserted above with caret*
[12] dydst] dost *altered to* dydst ("y" *inserted into word after first* "d" *and* "o" *modified to second* "d")

Nor hope[13] of future *good* will backe detaine. /
B: And longe may they remaine, I humbley pray,
For they remaining, howsoever waves
Of woe my *ship* shall tosse, I shall swime out. /
45   But[14] yet how much from former *dignity*
Hereby I am disgraded° you may see.
Ph: Somewhat wth thee I see wee have p[re]vailed
In y^t in mynd thou art not whole deiected,
Yet may not I thy nicenes° suffer longe. /   12 [r]
50   In y^t some great defect of happines
In mornefullwise thou dost as yet deplore. /
ffor who is seated so in setled state,
Who will not blame sometymes sinister fate. /
Crossed wth cares is mans most cheife content,
55   W^ch eith[er] will not whole to one become,
Or els will not endure still permanent.
One *man* in wealth doth wallow, whom base bloud
Obscureth much. Anoth[er] *noblenes*
Of bloud doth blaze abroad, yet povertie
60   Restraining him, hee seekes to live[15] obscure /
Anoth[er] havinge wealth and noble bloud
The want of wedlocke wailes. Another man
Havinge a vertuous wife, doth children want,
Who heapeth riches up for oth[er] men. /
65   Anoth[er] having *iſſue*, yet wth teares
His sonne or daughters want of grace bewailes. /
Hence none wth their estate do rest content. /
For many things men knowe not till they try,
W^ch havinge proved they detestinge fly. /
70   Moreover in mans prosperous estate
Their sence is passinge delicate and nice,° /
Unles at hartes desire all things succede,
Because they are not wont to any crosse,
W^th trifles small their mynd surprised is.
75   So litle lets do interrupt the state
Of them, who seeme to be most fortunate.

---

[13] hope] "o" *deleted after* "o" *MS*
[14] But] *inserted in left margin*
[15] live] secure *deleted after* live *MS*

How many live, who would in world of ioyes
Themselves account, if of the relickes left
Of thine estate, they might least part enioye?
80   This very place wch thou *exile* dost call,
To the *Inhabitants* is *native* soyle,
For nothinge I do miserable deeme,
Save y^t w^{ch} *mans* conceite doth so esteeme.
Contrarywise all states are good to men,
85   If *man* endure them wth a patient mynd.
Who is so *fortunate* wch would not wishe
In his impatiency, his state to change?
Wth many bitter pills *mans* best estate
Thoughe seeminge sweete, is sawced now and then,
90   W^{ch} thoughe to him who doth the same enioye
It pleasant show, yet when it will depart
Cannot by any means retained be.
Wherfore all mortall creatures happines
Mixed wth miserie, imperfect is,
95   W^{ch} constant staies not, wth mynds patient:
Nor mynds perplexed doth at all content.   [12 v]
Why then (*o mortall men*) in outward things
Felicitie, wch is internall set
Wthin yo[ur] mynds, do you so fondly seeke?
100   Error and ignorance yo[ur] sence confound. /
Of cheife felicitie the roote and springe
I here will breifly showe. Is anythinge
To thee, then is thy selfe, more precious?
Thou wilt say nothinge: then unles thy mind
105   Rashly distracted thee, thou shalt possesse
What never thou wilt afterward forgoe,
Or fortune can from thee by force surprice.°
And y^t in such fraile things thou maist conceive
Felicity cannot consist. Thus prove
110   *Yf happines be natures sovereigne good*,
And y^t may not be counted *happines*
W^{ch} from thee any way may be depriv'd,
Because what cannot faile is demed best:
Tis plaine that *fortunes* instabilitie,
115   Cannot attaine to true felicitie. /
Further whom such fraile happines extolls,

Her changinge state he eithr doth perceive,
Or els therof he must be ignorant.
Yf he be ignorant, what *happines*
120 Where *ignorance* remains, may wee expect?
But if he knowe it, then he must needs feare
Lest, what hee knowes is mutable, he lose,
So endles feare bereaves his *happines*. /
Suppose if one it loose, he should esteeme
125 The same to be dispised as a toy,
In such case it were but a simple good,
W^ch being lost must not of worth be waighed. /
And thou because by sundry arguments
Thy mynd I knowe resolved is y^t soules
130 Of mortall men end not wth bodies death:
And whereas it is clear, that death doth end
All worldlie happines wch man can have,
It may not be denied, if *death* bereave
Felicity, then men by meanes of *death*
135 In miserable case[16] are wretched made. /
But sith we knowe by *death* and tortures rage
Many have wisely sought for *happines,*

How can this p[re]sent life men happie make,
W^ch wretched makes not them who life forsake? /

Meter 4 ·   13 /[r]

What man so ever will wisely his house erect,
Contrivinge it with skill firme to resist the wind:
And seated so to stand, as waves it may reiect,
On hills or thirsty sand, no safe place can he find.
5   *Mountaines by windes unsure to him will yeild no place:*
      Nor sinkinge Sandes endure to beare great weight long space. /

Remember, if you would both dangers these eschew,
The firme meane rock to hould, where build not over highe:
Though windes, or Surginge Seas threat ruins to ensue,
10   *Yet thou in quiet ease as in a towre shalt ly:*
      Secure wth such defense, waled on every syde,
      All sturdy stormes offence safly thou maist deride. /

---

[16] case] "u" *deleted after* "a" *MS*

Prose 5 /

But for so much into thy mynd more deepe
My arguments descend (now medicine
More forcible to use I iudge it fitt)[17]
Admit these gifts of *fortune* were not frayle
5   What is there in wch may be counted thine
Or wch observed duly is not base?
Are riches p[re]cious in regard of yo[ur]
Or of their *nature*? What in them is great?
Whether is gould and monyes heapes of price?
10   But gould by spendinge doth his valew showe
Much rather then by hould fast hordinge up. /
For averice doth make men odious,
But bounty allwaies maketh glorious.
Now if wth man y^t cannot longer stay
15   W^{ch} unto others use translated is,
Mony then worthy is, when from thy self
To others use it is transferred cleane.
Yf wealth of all the world by one alone
Were hoarded, oth[ers] all would poor become,
20   And wth one voice all would alike bewayle.
Yo[ur] wealth also, save by diminishing,
To many cannot parted be at once:
W^{ch} beinge done it needs them poor must make
Who unto oth[ers] do the same in part.
25   O slender then and nedie is such wealth,
Whom many neith[er] wholely can enioy,
Nor any but by other mens anoy:
Do glitteringe *gemmes* transparent eies delight?
Yf in their brightnes any worth appeare,
30   There light to them, and not to men, belonge. /   [13 v]
Whom I admyre, to see men so esteeme.
ffor what thinge wantting soule, and members frame
Of livinge reasonable creatures ought,
Rightlie to be esteemed beautifull?
35   W^{ch} though by reason of *Gods* wisdome deepe
In their creation and theire formes distinct
Some beauty small they have, yet far below

---

[17] fitt)] fitt *MS*

Yo[ur] worth, should not at all be honoured soe.
Doth beauty of the feilds yo[ur] mynd delight?
40   *Bo*: Why not? Wheras it is a porc[i]on faire
Of the most beautifull created world,
So, to behould calme *Seas* we oft reioyce,
So firmament and twinkling starres to view,
The *Sunne and Moone* wee likewise do admyre.
45   *Ph*: Doth anyone of these thy selfe concern?
Or in theire *glory* wilt thou vainely boast?
Wth fragrant vernall flowers art thou adorn'd?
Dost thou the *Sommers* fruitfullnes procure?
Wth vaine delights, why art thou so deceav'd?
50   Externall goods for thine why dost thou count?
Fortune can never cause these to be thine,
W^{ch} *nature* from thy selfe estranged hath.
The *fruites* of *earth*, wthout all doubt, are made
Creatures wth nurrishment for to sustaine.
55   But if to helpe you, *Natures* wants you crave,
Fortunes abundance never wish you have.
ffor *Nature* is wth litle things content.
Whom if wth things superfluous you loade,
Unpleasant, or els hurtfull to thy selfe
60   It will become, wch is more then enough.
Perhapps in change of garments p[re]cious
To be attired goodly show doth seeme,
Wherof if any ornament appeare
Unto the nature of the stuffe, or els
65   Unto the workemans witt the praise is due.
Doth servants ample traine thee happie make,
Who if they vicious be, unto thy howse
Pernicious burden are, and to the lord
Therof, exceedinge enimies, they prove.
70   Yf vertuous they be, there worthines
To be thy *goodes* how canst thou make account?
Hereby y^t none of these are thine appeares,
W^{ch} thou amongst thy goods esteemed hast
Wherin if *goodnes* none remain to have them,
75   Why dost thou waile their want, or ioy to save them.   14 ·[r]
But if by *nature* these are beautifull,
What is y^t unto thee? For of themselves

These had ben as delightfull every way,
Yf from thy *goodes* they had been sequestred.
80   Neither they therfore are more p[re]cious,
Because they were amongst thy former wealth:
But rath[er], in y^t they did worthy seeme,
Amongst thy substance thou didst them account.
But what wth such turmoyle do you require?
85   I thinke wth wealth yo[ur] wants to ease you seeke. /
But oth[er]wise wth you it falleth out.
ffor many helps men neede, a sumptuous howse
Wth rich variety for to maintaine.
And true is this, y^t many things those want,
90   Who many things possesse. And lesse they neede,
Who measure theire abundance by necessity
Of *nature,* not regardinge superfluitie. /
Is no internall *good* ordayned you
By *nature,* y^t in such externall things
95   Yo[ur] cheifest *goodes* to seeke you enterprice?
So should the course of things perverted be
Y^t so divine a creature as is man
Endu'd wth reason, should not happie be
But by the use and sole possession
100   Of goods externall, wanting vitall life. /
All creatures els wth *nature* rest content.
But you whose mynd like to[18] *Gods* image shines,
From basest things do covet ornaments
To make you happie, neith[er] do you knowe,
105   What wronge to yo[ur] *creator* hence doth growe.
Above all creatures he mankind would grace,
But you p[re]fer such trash as is most base.
ffor if of every thinge the cheifest *good*
More worthie be, then is the thing it self:
110   Wheras yo[ur] good, the base things you account
Yo[ur] selves to them, as baser, you submit. /
W^{ch} not unworthely doe come to passe,
For this of humaine *nature* is the state
That then alone, when man him selfe doth knowe
115   All creatures els by much he doth surmount:

---

[18] to] *inserted above with caret*

But if this state to understand he cease
Inferior unto beasts he doth become. /
Nature to beastes their state would never showe,
But man ought perfectlie him selfe to knowe.
120 How farre doth *error* yo[urs] it selfe extend?   [14 v]
In y^t wth oth[er] ornaments so strange,
A thing may be adorned you esteeme, /
But y^t may by no meanes effected be. /
For if in things externall, worthines
125 Doth showe it selfe, the praise to them belongs.
And whatsoever is their wth adorned
Remaineth (not wthstanding such attire)
Not changed from the former base estate. /
Moreov[er] I deny such thing is *good*, /
130 W^{ch} hurteth him who doth the same enioy. /
Is this untruth I speake? You will say, no. /
But riches often times do damnifie
Those men, who have them in possession.
Wheras bad men, the skume of all mankind
135 Who after other mens possessions gape,
What gould or iewells may atchived be
Account them only worthiest of all,
Who do such vanities in store possesse.
Thou then who ever speare and sword dost feare
140 Wth doubtfull dread, if in this vale of life
An empty passinger thou haddest been
Careles[19] before a theife thou migh'st have songe
  O worthy happines of riches sure
  Which when men have they leave to live secure. /

      Meter 5 /
Thrice happie was the old forepassed tyme,
Which with manuringe of ground was content,
No prodigalities consuminge cryme
Was seene, but acornes oft for meate were[20] spent:
5 *When wine wth hony boyled was not used,*
  When purple silke for garments was refused.

---

[19] Careles] *word deleted before* Careles *MS*
[20] were] *two letters deleted after* "w" *with first* "e" *inserted above*

Grasse then instead of beds sweete sleepe did give,
Rivers did give drinke fitt for men to live. /

The pine trees shadow then gave place to dwell,
10   *No marchant then adventured so far:*
Strange marchendize for to transport to sell
No trumpets call did summon then to warre. /
    No bloudy battails nourished by hate.
    For why should warlike furie move debate?
15   *When woundes by warie wisdome men did see*
    No recompence of bloudshed for to be.   15 /[r]

O would to God that our declininge age
Would now encline unto such manners old:
But covetouse²¹ desire doth range and rage,
20   *Like Ætna's fire, possessions more to hould. /*
    In former tymes what wretched man, alas,
    Of goulden mines the first inventor was?
    Or whose device first needles iewels found,
    Which dangers are of price longe hid in ground? /

Prose 6 · /
Concerninge *dignities* and princelie powers,
W^ch you, not knowinge true *Renowne and might*,
To heaven do extole, what *should* I speake?
Who if ungodlie man attaine to have,
5   What harm by *Ætna's* flashinge flames more greate,
Or overflowinge flouds more havocke make?
Doubtles (as I suppose thou dost remember)
Yo[ur] Ancesto[urs], the *Consulls* government,
W^ch of theire freedome was originall,
10   For their exceedinge pride abolish would.
Who for like pride before would not²² sustaine
The name of *Kinge* over their state to reigne.
But if (wch is full rare) on worthie man
Honours imposed are for their desert,
15   What oth[er] thinge in them admyred is,

---

²¹ covetouse] "u" *deleted after* "t" *MS*
²² would not] *inserted above with caret*

Except their *vertues* wch they exercise?
Wherby it comes to passe that *dignitie*
To *vertue* doth not *honour* give at all:
But rath[er] unto worldlie *dignities*,
20   From vertue princelie *honour* doth pertaine. /
What is this pompous power wch you wish[?]
Do not you²³ understand (*o mortall men*):
Over how seely° things you seeme to raigne?
For if amongst the *Mice* someone to claime
25   Title or maiestie amongst the rest
Thou didst espie, couldst thou refraine to laugh? /
Now if mans body you respect aright
What thinge more impotent, then wretched man
Can you find out? Whom often smallest flies,
30   By bitinge or by crepinge into them
Through inward passages do hurt or slay. /
And can mans puißaunce further extend
Over their subiects then²⁴ the body sole,   [15 v]
And over y^t wch is inferior
35   To bodies much? (their substance fraile I meane)
Mans free will to thy scepter canst thou tame?
A mynd by reason firme established
From state of constant resoluc[i]on,
Art thou by *force* able for to remove?
40   When on a tyme a *Tyrant* purposed
Wth punishments, a worthie constant man
To force, conspiraces complotted there
By some against his person to bewraye:°
His tounge the man did bite from out his mouth,
45   And in the face of raginge *Tyrant* threw. /
So tortures wch the *Tyrant* ment to make
The meanes to practize savage cruelty,
That constant man made to expresse fidelity. /
And what can man against a man effect,
50   W^{ch} by anoth[er] may not be repaid?
Busiris (as the *histories* record)
Accustomed him selfe his guests to slay,

---

²³ you,] you *MS*
²⁴ then] *inserted above with caret*

At last by *Hercules* his guest was slain. /
The *Carthaginian captives* not a fewe,
55   Though *Regulus* had into prison cast,
Captive to them yet shortlie he became.
Then thinkest thou such man can be of power,
Who what he can to other men effect,
Others likewise may backe to him repaie?
60   Further if in *Renowne* and princlie power
Were any naturall and proper good,
Unto bad men they never would descend.
For in things contrary no concord is,
Their *nature* is not to concurre in one.
65   Then for so much as often wicked men
To honourable place wee see are called
Nature doth not y^t to be *good* account,
W^{ch} wth *bad men* is wont for to remaine. /
W^{ch} thinge to all *dame fortunes* ornaments
70   May not unworthelie imputed bee.
W^{ch} commonlie to the most naughtie men
In more abundant sort imparted are.
Concerninge whom this is to be observ'd,
That no man doubts such one is valiant
75   In whom a mynd couragious doth appeare:
Who swiftnes hath is to be counted swifte.   16 /[r]
So musicks skill maketh *Musitians*.
Knowledge of phisicke doth *Phisitians* make,
And skill rethoricall an *Orator*.
80   For *nature* in all things doth y^t effect
W^{ch} unto everythinge peculiar is.
Neith[er] doth *she*, effects of div[ers] things
Repugnant in them selves, rashly confound,
But things wch are in *Nature* contrary
85   *She* allwaies warily distinguisheth:
But riches neith[er] quench mans avarice,
Nor rule can make such man him selfe to rule
Whom lawles lusts in fetters firm retaine.
And *hono[urs]* on bad men imposed, oft
90   Therby they do not more renowned grow,
But rath[er] their unworthines do showe.
How cometh this so strange event to passe?

For you, such names unfit to many things
W^{ch} are in truth unworthie of the same
95   Are wont to give, wch by their owne effects
Theire greate indignity them selves bewray.°
So neith[er] riches yo[urs] are wealth in truth,
Nor mortall powre may be esteemed might,
Nor *dignity* of man doth worthely
100   Deserve the name of *hono^r*, duly stand:
Lastlie concerninge *fortunes goodes* ech one
The same I may conclude, wherin tis plaine
Nothinge deserveth to be wished much,
Neith[er] therin is any *native good*
105   For to *good men* they are not allwaies prest,
Nor make *men good* wth whom they most do rest.

Meter 6 · /
Wee know what ruines Nero Tyrant wrought.
Rome by him burn'd and Senators were slayne,
Brother he slew securely for to raigne,
In mothers wombe this bloudy boucher sought
5   *To view the place whence hee to world was brought,*
Not greiv'd to see her shame and death sustain. /

Yet Realmes this Tyrant rul'd with mighty mace
Which are dispersed farre from East²⁵ to west:
Cold North, and skorchinge South he had possest.
10   *Could then this monsters mynd, in any case*
Corrected be, by havinge princely place?
O, happ most hard were bloudy Tyrants rest. /   [16 v]

Pro: 7 ·
B: You knowe that arrogant ambition
Of *Kingdomes* rule hath not me over rul'd
But the occation fit to be employ'd
In the affaires of native com[m]on wayle
5   I did desire, lest in obscurity
Vertue unexercised hid should ly. /
Ph: Doubtles this is a thinge wch worthy mynds

---

²⁵ East] *letter deleted after "E" MS*

By *Nature*, yet not brought to ripenes full
Of *vertues* habit, quicklie may alure,
10   Namely desire of glorious name, and fame
Of great deserts, on common wealth bestowed. /
W^ch of how slender reputac[i]on
Voyd of all weight it is, I argue thus:
That all the earth compared to the skies,
15   (As demonstrac[i]on Astrologicall
Hath heretofore at large instructed thee)
Hath but proporc[i]on of a pricke, tis plaine: /
So as if you respect of heavens globe
The spacious, and ample magnitude,
20   The earth as nothinge in account doth seeme.
And scarce the fourth parte^26 of this little earth
(As *Ptolomeus* hathe thee lately taught)
By livinge creatures wch are to us known,
Remaineth at this day inhabited,
25   If from this fourth part you in mynd subtract
So much as *Seas* and marshes overflowe,
And parts inhabitable made by heate,
Most narrow space where men inhabiteth^27
Will then remain in this subtraction^28
30   Then if in least point of so^29 slender bounds
Environed you are, to spreade yo[ur] fame
Or blaze abroad yo[ur] name whie do you seeke?
Can fame and ample glory their remayne
Wher earthes streight lymets do the same containe?
35   Moreover in this narrow mansion place
Inhabit many *nations* different
In tounge, in manners, and in course of lyfe,
To whom both^30 for the dangers of the way,
And for the disagreing languages,
40   As allso for the want of trafficks use,
Not only fame of private men can fly

---

26 parte] "r" *inserted above with caret*
27 inhabiteth] te *inserted above with caret*
28 subtraction] "i" *inserted above with caret*
29 so] *inserted above with caret*
30 both] "o" *deleted after* "o" *MS*

But also famous citties are unknowne. /
In *Tullies* tyme, as he him selfe doth writ,   17 [r]
The fame of *Romaine Empire* glorious,
45   Beyond *Mount Caucasus* had not been heard:[31]
W^{ch} not wthstandinge unto *Parthians* spread,
And *Nations* neare adioyninge feared was.
Wherfore dost not thou understandinge see
How narrow bounds do glorious name include:
50   W^{ch} men to propagate and spreade contend?
Sith fame could not transporte the *Romaine* name,
How should a private *Romaine* seek the same?
Furth[er] the lawes and manners disagree
In divers countries: so what some com[m]end,
55   Others as punishment deservinge will condemne.
Wherby it comes to passe if ample fame
Dispersed wide shall any man delight
In[32] cuntries distant farre to blaze his name
By no meanes shall availeable become.
60   Wherefore contented every man must rest
Amongst his owne to have his glory spread,
Whose cheife renowned immortallitie
Wthin *one Nations* bounds must curbed be.
How many men in theire daies most admyred
65   Hath now oblivions most ungratefull vice,
In silence buried thorough writers faulte?
Yet what can histories wth glory crowne,
Whom wth their *Authors* tract of tyme will drowne?
But you, *o men*, to sowe immortall seeds
70   A name unto yo[ur] selfe supposinge seeme,
When future[33] fame you doe propound to reape.
But if wth tymes eternity you would
Make the comparison, what reason then
Of names continuance have you to boast?
75   For why? One moment, to tenn thowsande yeares
Yf you compare, beinge both[34] finit tymes,

---

³¹ heard] "e" *inserted above*
³² In] "n" *inserted above with caret*
³³ future] futrue *MS*
³⁴ both] "o" *deleted after* "o" *MS*

They have, though smale, yet some proporc[i]ons place:
But all those yeares, or many thowsand more,
Respectinge endles tymes continuance,
80   Have not at all comparison. For why
Betwen things finite, is proporc[i]on some,
But not betwen things infinite at all. /
So longest fame, compared to eternity,
Not only small, but nothinge seemes to be. /
85   Most men, unles base popularity,
And rumors vaine did haughty harts incite,
Would not attempt exploits of good reporte:
But leavinge conscience and vertues worth,
From sillie fames bare words do seeke reward.
90   Behould such arrogance³⁵ and vainest pride   [17 v]
How pleasantly one taunting did deride.
When he another man abused had
Who not for vertues sake, but glories pride,
Would be esteemed a *Philosopher:*³⁶
95   And havinge added he would shortlie try
Wheth[er] a right *Philosopher* he were indeed,
For then he would, w^{th}out impatience,
All offred iniuryes gentle sustaine. /
The man him selfe a while wth patience arm'd,
100   At last insultinge over such reproche,
How dost thou not, said he, perceive I am
A right *Philosopher?* The other then
In quippinge sort thus girded at his brage.°
I had perceiv'd³⁷ you to be such a one,
105   Yf you yo[ur] silence had continued. /
But what unto those excellentest men,
(Of them I speake who fame by vertue seeke)
What parte of fame, I say, doth after death
To them pertaine? Put case° men wholely dy
110   Both soules and bodies, (wch my arguments
Soundly confute) no glory then at all
To them can appertaine, because the man

---

³⁵ arrogance] arogancy *MS*
³⁶ *Philosopher*] *Pholosopher MS*
³⁷ perceiv'd] "e" *deleted after* "v" *MS;* perceiv'd] perceivd *MS*

Whose fame is celebrated and extoll'd
Hath no existence in the world at all. /
115   But if the unpolluted soule of man
Dissolved from the bodies prison base,
Into the heavens freely doth ascend:
  Earthlie *Renowne* will not that soule despice,
  From earth exempt, enioying happie *skies?*

Meter 7

Who glory rashly requireth or only recounteth a cheife gemme,
If he revolve but a right comparinge hugenes of heavens
With litle earth verie like to a point, in quanty smalest,
Then to reioyce of a name advanced on earth is a madnes. /
5 *Why do the proude meditate to reiect mortallity vainely?*
Though very farre glory spreade to the furthest corner in all costs,
Also thy howse title hould very high, Death vaine glory skorneth
Endeth alike all states myseries with dignity matchinge. /
Where be the bones to be seen of worthy Fabricius? And where
10 *Now doth abide noble Brutus? Or else wary Cato severest?*
Name naked only remaines that in history resteth of all these. /
But to what end sely° names can availe? Can a dead body know them?
Dead men, alas, do not heare, nor fame can againe so recall them.
But if you count it a life to be keept by the voice of a vaine name,
15 *Names memory perishing in tyme: Death endeth againe fame.*

    Prose 8 · /   18 [r]
But lest I over feirce seeme to wage warr
Against *dame fortune, she* sometymes, I grant,
Of men to be com[m]ended doth deserve.
Namely when *she* her visage doth unmaske,
5 And doth *her nature* manifestly show. /
Perchaunce what I pronounce you skarce perceive.
A wonder here I purpose to relate,
But words my meaninge to disclose I want
For more available I iudge *adversity,*
10 For man, then *fortunes* steps in proud *prosperity.*
For vaine *prosperity* under p[re]tence
Of true felicity, marchinge in pompe[38]

---

[38] pompe] *whole word over-written in darker ink*

Doth counterfeit, wth vaine dißemblinge showes.
Adversity, simplicity retains,
15   Who showes her state unstable still to³⁹ change,
The *one* deceiveth, th'oth[er] doth instruct.
The *one* under true gooddnes⁴⁰ painted vaile
Bewitcheth mynds of men who *her* enioy:
The oth[er] doth man free, instructing him
20   That mortall happines inconstant is.
Wherefore the one to be fraile, wavering,
And ignorant of her inconstancy,
You may observe: wheras *adversity*
Is sober, discret, and by exercise
25   In miseries affaires, becometh wise.
Lastlie prosperities by flatteries
From soveraigne happines seduceth man
Adversity wthdraweth oft the mynd
Reducinge man felicity to finde.
30   Dost thou this *good* amongst the least account,
That frowninge *fortune* by her austere chaunge
Who were thy freinds unfained hath reveal'd?
She hath distinguished betwen thy freinds,
And fawninge foes, *she* hath discovered
35   Wheras thy former vaine prosperity
Departinge from thee, *she unconstant* harts
Removed hath, leavinge thy freinds unfain'd.
What wouldest thou have given so to know
Thy freinds from foes, when y^t, as thou dost iudge,
40   Thy *state* did florish fortunate appearing?⁴¹
      Cease then to wail the losse of wealth so sore. /
      Freinds thou hast found the derest riches store. /

Meter 8
Divine love, moderatinge earth and seas,
Who also highest heavens guidinge swayes,
Such order doth in Natures courses tye: [18 v]
That therby permanent the world doth stand,

---

³⁹ to] *word deleted after* to *MS*
⁴⁰ gooddnes] *letters over-written as* dd *in darker ink*
⁴¹ appearing?] *","* *deleted with* *"?"* *inserted above*

5   Changinge the seasons wth a stable hand,
       That every tyme succeds in harmony.

       That Elements, who are repugnant farre,
       In fellowship concordinge cease from iar,°
       Whose naturall instinct would else have fought:
10   That dawninge day returnes by Phœbus light,
       That Phœbe governeth the starry night,
       Which Hesperus had in the evening brought. /

       That swellinge Sea doth boystrous billowes keepe,
       Containinge them in lymitts of the deepe,
15   So as earthes boundes it may not overflowe:
       This love divine, if raines it should remitt,
       The things wch now by naturall love are knitt,
       Debate disorderinge soone would overthrowe. /

       And heavens frame wch orderly doth move
20   Combined with sweete sosiable love,
       To ruine desolate would come, and end:
       This love doth people in firme leauge contain
       United wth inviolable chaine,
       This love doth wedlockes bounds syncere defend.

25   Lastly this love betwixt true freinds doth cause
       Uncounterfeited frindships constant lawes,
       Without dissemblinge gloses firme to bide:
       O happie thrice it were unto mankind
       If such love would vouchsafe to rule mans mynd,
30   Which heavens motions all doth firmely guide.

THE · PHYSICKE [1] · OF · PHILOSOPHIE [2]
compiled by Anicius Manlius Torquatus
Severinus Boethius touchinge
the consolation of Lady
Philosophie in the
tyme of his exile /

The third booke contayninge stronger receipts purginge
forceably his errors shewing also wherin true ~ ~
happines consisteth /

The first prose · /

B: Her sonnet then *she* ended, when delight
Of verses sweete my mynd so ravished,   19 [r]
That still attentive more to heare, I stoode.
Wherfore a litle afterwards I sayd:[3] /
5   O sollace swetest unto feeble mynds
Wth gravest sentences and harmony
How much have you my troubled mynd refrest!
So as wth *fortunes* forces, I now iudge
My selfe, for to encounter, not unfitt. /
10   And phisicke wch before was sowre, you said,
I hunger to receive nothinge dismay'd. /
P. I knewe thy thoughts, said *she*, when first I sawe
My words attentively thou didst observe.
W^{ch} state of mynd I partlie did expect,
15   In thee (or to speake truth) I did procure. /
For remydies remaininge are as gall
Bitter in tast, but yet received sweete.

---

[1] *PHYSICKE*] "c" *inserted above with caret and written in darker ink*
[2] *Philosophie*] *second "h" inserted above with caret;* **THE PHYSICKE OF**
PHILOSOPHIE] *THE PHYSICKE OF PHILOSOPHIE MS*
[3] sayd:] sayd. *MS*

But you in y^t to hear, you say, you thirst
How would yo[ur] kindled coles more ardent growe
20   Yf whith[er] I you leade you plaine did knowe?
Bo: Whith[er] said I?^{4} *P*. To true felicitie
Quoth *she*, wherof thy mynd hath also dream'd
But sith thine eies vaine shadowes dazeled have,
Clearely the truth you cannot yet behould.
25   *Bo*: Leade me, said I entirelie I you praye,
And happie truth to me wth speede reveale.
Ph: Gladly, said *she*, for thy sake will I shew
Wherin felicity consisteth true.
But seeminge truth wch nearer is to thee
30   I first in words will here delineate
W^{ch} when you shall apparantly perceive,
      And shall to contraries yo[ur] mynd adresse,
      You may conceive what is true happines. /

Meter 1 /

Who so will sowe
His fertil land,
Letteth not weede
Theirin remaine:
5   *Nor lets briers growe,*
Nor ferne to stand,
That he may speede
Of store of graine.
      The hony tast more pleasant bringes
10   *Yf first thou hast feedd of sowre thinges. /*   [19 v]

The starres do shine
More gratefully,
When Southren winde
Doth cease to raigne,
15   *Aurora fine*
Adornes the sky
When darknes blinde
Is cleansed cleane.

---

^{4} I?] I. *MS*

So shalt thou see first goods untrue,
20   *After to thee true goodes ensue.* /

Prose 2 · / ·

She stedfast fixinge then awhile *her* eies,
And as it were retyringe all her thoughts
Into the secret closet of *her* mynd,
She thus begun[n]e. *P*: All care of mortall man
5   W^ch he by studie manifold doth take
In pathes most different doth marchinge goe,
Yet not w^thstandinge to a happie state
Mans mynd endeavoureth still to attaine,
W^ch *goodnes* is, wch if a man atcheive
10   None can require to gaine a furth[er] end.
For this of all *good* things cheifest doth rest
And doth therin all *good thinges* else containe.
Wherin if want theire were, it were not best,
Because somethinge externall it should want.
15   Then *happines* is such a perfect state
Where all *good thinges* concurre most fortunate. /
This, as I said, all men doe seeke to have,
But yet one path men do not theire to take,
For naturall desire and inclinac[i]on
20   To cheifest good in man engrafted is,
But them to vanities *error* doth leade.
Wherof some men accountinge happines
Nothinge to want, in wealth seeke to abound
Some iudginge *honours* true felicitie,
25   Of Cittizens to be saluted strive.
Some placinge *happines* in princely power,
Will eyth[er] have the scepter in their hand,
Or Princes favourits will ayme to bee. /
Oth[ers] who fame renowned most esteeme
30   By skill in warr or peace to celebrate
His glorious name to skies endevoureth. /   20 [r]
Most men their cheifest *good* by ioy do measure,
Who take *delight* to wallow in their pleasure. /
Some these ends seeke one for anothers sake,
35   As those who riches covet to attaine
That theirby power and pleasures they may wyn,

Or els who power requier for riches sake,
Or to advance their fame uppon the earth. /
In these and in such like the whole intent
40   And scope of humaine actions, and desires
Alone consisteth, as *nobility*
And *favour* populer, wch may to *fame*
And *glory* be referred properly,
A wife[5] and children for sweete pleasure are
45   Of *men* so much desired[6] and embraced.
And freinds wch are most sacred lincke of all
In vertue not in *fortune* I repute,
All oth[er] acc[i]ons man doth undertake
Either for power, or els for pleasures sake.
50   Now for the bodies goods tis evident
That to the former kinds they may be brought
For strength and stature great resemble power,
Bewtie and nimblenes a glorious fame,
Soundnes of health may be refer'd to pleasure. /
55   Of all whom only true *felicity*
Is aymed at, and wished, it is plaine.
For, what above all oth[er] things wee wish,
That thinge as *goodnes* principall we count.
But *goodnes* cheife, to be *beatitude*
60   Before wee have recounted and defined
Wherefore above the rest what one requireth,
That counting *happines* he most desireth.[7] /
Before thine eies the forme of happie state
In some sort have I sett to be beheld
65   Namely *wealth, honour, maiestie, glory,*
And pleasures wch the *Epicurean* sect
Solely considering, by consequence
Pleasure to be cheife *good*, did rashly deeme.
Because the other all into the mynd
70   *Pleasure* to yeild doth manifestlie seeme. /
But to mans drifts I now againe retourne,[8]

---

[5] wife] "e" *deleted after* "w" *MS*
[6] desired] "o" *deleted after* "i" *MS*
[7] desiereth] "o" *deleted after* "i" *MS*
[8] retourne,] retourne. *MS*

Whose mynds affection, thoughe, the memory
Obscured be, doth wish *good* principall.
But as a drunkard doth not knowe wch way   [20 v]
75   Hom to his howse he maye him selfe convaye. /
So doth those err who seke sufficiency?
Doubtles to happie state no other thinge
Can more availe then plenty of all *good*
Not wanttinge other helpes, but for it selfe.
80   Having enoughe. Either do such men err
Who iudge what thinge is best, deserveth most
Wth reverence to be saluted? No. /
Nor can it be a base and abiect thinge
W^{ch} to enioy most mortall men aspire. /
85   And is not power to be counted *good?*
What els? Can it be weak and without power
W^{ch} more in worth,⁹ then all beside, we count. /
Is glorious name to be as nothing thought?
But questionles what is most p[re]cious
90   Wee must esteeme to be most glorious.
What shall I say that true *beatitude*
Is neither pensive nor subiect to greife.
For in least things man seeketh to enioy
Unto the mynd what is delightful most. /
95   These are the things wch men require to gaine
Who for these causes ardentlie desire
*Riches, Renowne, Realmes, glory, and delight.*¹⁰
Because herby they thinke they maye attaine
Abundance, Honour, Puissance, fame, and ioye
100   Then it is *good* wch men by divers meanes
So much do covet, wherein see the force
          Of *nature.* Though mens Iudgments div[ers] be,
          In choice of *goodnes* end yet all agree. /

Meter 2 · /

My muse in sonnet meaneth to declare
What reines of rule Nature in things ordeyned,
And in what order all by her conteyned

---

⁹ worth] wealth *deleted with* worth *inserted above*
¹⁰ *delight*] second Renowne *deleted with* delight *inserted above*

United wth stronge chaine unchanged are. /

5   Though lyons lye in chaines receivinge meate
From keepers handes, whose stripes he often beareth,
Yet keeper first wth bloudy tooth he teareth
Burstinge his boundes by Natures raginge heate. /

The chirpinge birde wch singes in height of tree,   21 [r]
10   Contain'd¹¹ in cage, and keept wth keepers care,
Allthough with foode most delicate she fare,¹²
Preferreth wonted woodes, and Liberty.

The top of sturdy plants bended wth strength,
When hould you leave, it selfe upright will raise:
15   Phœbus doth dip his beames in westerne Seas,
Yet under earth returnes to East at length. /

All things reioyce in Natures order sure,
All thinges on courses certaine do depend:
And do delight, to come to proper end,
20   Whereby the world doth constantly endure. /

Prose 3 · /

And you, o earthlie creatures, in some sort
Imperfectlie of yo[ur] begin[n]inge dreame:
Also yo[ur] end *felicitie*, in parte
Allthoughe not plainely, you conceive and see. /
5   And thither you by *naturall* instinct
Are caried, but blind *error* manifould
From thence seduceth unto vanities. /
For marke if by such meanes as men account
Their mynd to true beatitude can mount.
10   For if y^t *mony honour* or the rest
That no *good thinge* be wantinge, can performe,
Some man I also grant may by these meanes
To happie state attaine. But for as much
As these be neither to effect

---

¹¹ *Contain'd*] Containd MS
¹² *fare*] "e" deleted after "f" MS

15   What they do promise, and much *good* do want
       Is not therein vaine shewe of happines. /
       I first of you, who late in wealth did flowe,
       Do this demand, if in yo[ur] riches store
       Vexac[i]ons manifould you have not had
20   W^{ch} by some iniuries yo[ur] mynd made sad? /
       Bo: Doubtles said I, I cannot call to mynd
       That ever I remained long so free
       But y^t mishaps still crossing did me vex.
       Ph: Was not the cause said *shee*, y^t you did want
25   Such neceßaries as you would enioye?
       Or els because to use some thing as neare
       W^{ch} you would gladly have been furth[er] of?   [21 v]
       Bo: Yes verilie, said I. *P*: Then of the one
       The p[re]sence you, said *she*, desired,¹³ and
30   The oth[ers] absence. *B*: I confesse, said I.¹⁴
       P: And doth not man that want w^{ch} *he* doth wish?
       B: The same hee needs must want (then answered I)
       P: Now can such men who want to serve thire tournes
       Sufficiency be thought to harbour? *B*: No. /
35   *P*: You then quoth *she*, in wealth this want sustain'd.
       B: What then? said I. *P*: Then riches cannot make
       A man to have enough, and not to want,
       W^{ch} thinge to promise unto man they seeme.
       This also cheiflie may observed bee,
40   That *nature* gave not money force to save it
       But they perforce may lose the same who have it.
       B: I grant said I. *P*: Why should you not this graunt
       Sith daylie stronger men the same do take
       Wth violence from others of lesse might?
45   For whence ariseth pleadings in the lawe,
       And plaintiffs bills, but that they may recover
       Mony by force or fraude from them purloyn'd? /
       B: Most true, said I. *P*: Then man externall ayde
       To save his substance, wch he hath, doth want.
50   *B*: Who can deny the same? *P*: But others helpe

---

¹³ desired] "o" *deleted after* "i" *MS*
¹⁴ I.] I, *MS*

He had not needed but for monyes cause
W^{ch} he enioyed, wch els he might have lost.
B: No doubt said I. *P*: The case¹⁵ then altered is,
For wealth wch sem'd in nothing to be skant,
55   Needinge externall ayde, is still in want. /
But by what means can wealth yo[ur] wants expell?
For do not wealthy men hunger sustaine?
Are they not subiect unto thirst? Doth not
The winters frostie season rich men nipe?
60   But you will answer, that these wealthy men
Have where wth hunger, thirst, and cold t'expell:
Hereby I graunt their want may be releived,
But cannot so by them be quit removed.
For if by wealth be waylinge wants supplied,
65   Want still remaineth to be satisfied. /
I ceasc to showe y^t smale sufficeth *nature*,
But nothing can suffice the covetous.¹⁶ /
Wherfore if riches cannot wants remove:
    And if they want do cause, I marvaile much
70   Why men do place sufficcencye in such?   22 [r]

Met: 3 ·

Though rich men flowe
In surginge streames of gould,
Yet nigardes thirsty still,
Will never knowe
5   *Themselves¹⁷ ynough to hould,*
Their gredy want to fill. /

Though chaines abound
Brought from the Indies shore,
Of pearle and pretious stone,
10   *Though he much ground*
With hundred oxen store
Doth plough, yet will he grone:

---

¹⁵ case] "u" *deleted after* "a" *MS*
¹⁶ covetous] *letter deleted after* "t" *MS*
¹⁷ Themselves] selves *inserted above with caret*

And carkinge° care
Such men will never leave
15 *While as they be alive:*
Nor death will spare
Them wholely to bereave,
And them of goods deprive.

Prose 4 · /

B: But *dignities* to whom they shall befall
They make such worthy to be honoured. /
P: Hath *magistracy* might to make mans mynd
Abound in virtue, and abandon vice?
5   Doubtles it doth not evills put to flight
But rath[er] causeth *vice* it selfe to showe. /
From whence it is y^t wee do oft disdaine
That wicked men in highest places raigne.
ffor w^ch, *Catullus* calleth *Nonius*,
10 Sitting in iudgment seat, *Ill humors heape.* /
Do you not see what shame to wicked men
By *honour* com[m]eth? Whose unworthines[18]
Would lesse appeare, if in lowe state they were. /
And wouldest[19] thou for any dangers yeild
15 W^th *Decoratus* for to rule the state,
When thou in him didst plaine perceive a mynd
Of most base *Sycophants*, and pickthanke° vile?
Wee maye not iudge by reason of highe place
Those can deserve *Renowne*, whom wee esteeme   [22 v]
20 Unworthie of such place: but if you see
W^th wisdome any man to be endowed
Unworthie will you iudge him of *renowne*?
Or of his wisdom wch he hath? *B*: Not so.
For *honour* doth in vertue proper rest,
25 W^ch *she imparts* to her associats,
W^ch *hono[urs]* populer, cannot effect,
Wherefore they want the worth of *dignity.* /
Wherein this further may observed be.
For if a man be so much more abiect,

---

[18] unworthines] un *inserted above with caret*
[19] wouldest] "e" *inserted above with caret*

30   By how much more he is of men contemn'd:
      Sith royall place cannot make reverend,
      It rather wicked men more vile doth make,
      In y^t to many it doth showe their vice.
      But not for nought for wicked men restore
35   Againe like payment unto *dignities*,
      Whom they by vile contagion do pollute. /
      And y^t thou maist perceive that *honour* true
      By such vaine shadowes of a worthie place
      Cannot atchived be, I argue thus:
40   If any executinge *dignities*
      In cuntreys barbarous perhaps arive,
      Will *hono^r* past, strangers at all procure
      Wth reverence such men to entertaine?
      Surely if *hono[urs]* were to *dignities*
45   Guifts naturall, then in no cuntry strange
      To execute their office would they cease. /
      As fire in every coast endureth hoate. /
      But sith in them this is no proper force
      But mans opinion false supporteth it:
50   Before such men to banish they will seeme
      Who do not them as *dignities* esteeme. /
      But this I spoke concerninge cuntreys strange. /
      Now are they allwayes permanent wth those
      Who do inhabit in the selfe same land?
55   The *Pretors* office lately was of *might*,
      Only the name now vainely doth remain. /
      The *Senators* estate is tedious toil. /
      Yf any heretofore would oversee
      The peoples graine, such man was counted greate.
60   Now, then y^t office, what is thought more base?
      For, as wee said before, what inwardly   23 ·[r]
      Hath no *renowne*, receyveth worthines
      Or looseth it by mans opinion. /
      Yf *honours* then cannot men worthy make,
65   If they wax vile, by means of bad mens vice,
      If they in tract of tyme their worth forsake,
      If cuntreys strange esteeme them of no price,
           What beauty then therin can mans mynd move,
           Much lesse, before all, can deserve yo[ur] love. /

Meter 4 ·
Though Nero proud in prodigall excesse
Himselfe in Tyrian silke and gemmes did dresse,
Yet he most hatefull lived unto all
To Senators base dignities of late
5 *He did impart. Then honour from a state*
So abiect, who can truly happie call.

Prose 5 /
B: But cannot *Kingdomes* and the countenance
Of kings effect puissaunce absolute?
Why not? Wheras their endles happines
Constant wthout chaunge is conserved firme.
5 *P*: But auntient age examples many yeild
And later tymes wherin we live, declare
That *Kinges* felicitie inconstantly
Into extreame calamatie doth change.
O vaine is puissaunce, wch is unable
10 So much as the owne state to fortifie. /
Yf *kingdomes might* were cause of *happines*
Yf it on any part imperfect stand,
Would not such want diminish *happines*
Inferringe miserie? But yet allthough
15 *Kingdomes* terrestriall extend full far:
Cuntreys unconquered many remain
Over the wch no severall *Kinge* can raigne.
Now on what part *Kinges rule* is lymited
On y^t part impotencie entereth
20 W^{ch} curbinge their might doth them wretched make,
Deprivinge them of y^t, wch happie makes. /
Then in regard hereof *Kings* must poßesse
A greater part of woe than happines. /
A *Tyrant* havinge found in princely state
25 Dangers to lurke resembled *Kingdomes* feare
By hanginge of a sword above ones heade. /
What *maiestie* is this y^t cannot purge
Such biting cares nor stings of feare avoyde?[20]

---

[20] avoyde] *over-written in dark ink*

Doubtles they wish but cannot live secure:
30   And yet to boast of *might* they do not cease.
Dost thou him mightie iudge, whom souldiers ayde
Environeth[,] who whom he makes afraide   [23 v]
He feareth more him selfe whose strength dost stand
Not in him selfe but in his servants hand?[21]
35   What should I say of princes *favourits*
Sith *Kingdoms* imbecillitie[22] I showe?
These sometyme fall in kings prosperitie:
And vanish sometyme if the *kinge* do fail.
Nero constrained *Seneca* his freind
40   And *maister* to elect what *death* he would. /
Anthonius did obtrude *Papinian*
Mightie in court long tyme to souldie^rs sword.
Both[23] these did wish their highe place to renounce
Wherof grave *Seneca* to yeild his goods
45   Wholely to *Neros* will did iudge it best,
That he might spend his tyme in quiet ease. /
But whilst the greatnes of these *Tyrants* power
The slippery state of them did ruinate,
Neither effected y^t wch both[24] they sought.
50   What *might* is then wch they y^t have do feare?
W^ch when you wish to have you are not safe,
And when you wish to leave you cannot shune.
Are freinds a garrison whom vertues lincke
Hath not procured unto thee but chance?
55   But whom prosperitie hath made thy freind,
Successe unprosperous will make thy foe.
        What pestilence will then more dreadfull be,
        Then will be thyne familiar enymie? /

                    Meter 5 · /
        Who so true might would finde
        Must tame his lofty mynd.

---

[21] hand?] hand. *MS*
[22] imbecillitie] ti *inserted above with caret*
[23] both] "o" *deleted after* "o" *MS*
[24] both] "o" *deleted after* "o" *MS*

No lusts his thoughts must blind
                    Or hould in awe
5   *For though both*[25] *Indy land*
       And furthest Thule stand
       Subdued by thy hand
                    And feare thy lawe
       Yet that no might can be
10   *Which cannot cause to fly*
       Sharpe cares and misery
                    Which him do gnawe.

Prose 6 · /

How false is glory often and how vile?
Wherof *Tragedian* iustlie doth exclayme:
O glory, glory, to a thowsand men
Nothinge else made but vaine wind in the eare. /
5   ffore many men have falslie forged fame
From vaine opinion of the vulgar sort
More shamefull, then wch thing, what may be thought?   24 [r]
For who untrulie have a famous name
Needs must they blush at false reporte of fame. /
10   W^ch if by iust desert it were attained
Can *fame* availe to wise mens conscience?
Who measure not theire goods by peoples voice,
But by theire consciencies uprightnes.
But if to blaze o[ur] name be glorious,
15   Then not to spreade the same is odious.
But sith (as I before declared have),
Theire needs must be full many *Nations*
Wherto the fame of one man cannot fly,
It chaunceth y^t whom you iudge glorious,
20   In greatest part of earth shall be obscure. /
Moreover in such *fame* of common sort
I cannot see what can deserve *renowne*.
W^ch neither doth proceed to iudgement sound
Nor ever permanent to rest is found. /
25   Further how vaine and fraile is *noblenes*,
Of birth, who cannot see? W^ch if to *fame*

---

[25] *both*] "o" *deleted after* "o" *MS*

It be referred, it is not thire owne
For this, *nobilitie* doth seeme to be:
A praise from parents merit wch proceeds. /
30 Now if y^t praise makes noble, then such are,
To whom such praise is due, noble alone.
Wherfore yf in thy selfe be nothinge p[re]cious,
Anothers worth can never make thee glorious. /
Yf any good be in *nobilitie*,
35 It is in y^t on them necessity
     Imposed is, y^t they should not digresse
     From *vertue* of thir parents *noblenes*. /

Meter 6 · /

All humaine kind both²⁶ great and small
Ariseth from a like estate:
For why? One father is of all
Only directinge all by fate,
5   *He gave to Phœbus beames full bright,*
     To mone he gave²⁷ her hornelike light.

He granted man on earth t'abide,
He granted starres to rest in sky:
The soule in body he did hide
10 *Which did descend from heavens highe*
     Wherefore full honourable seede
     All mortall men at first did brede. /

Why then boast you of noble race?
If you would duly call to mynd,
15 *You all were made by divine grace,*
No man doth grow out of his kind,
     But he which doth vile vice embrace,
     Wherby he doth his birth deface. /   [24 v]

Prose 7 · /
What shall I say of bodies pleasure vaine?
Desire wherof is full of gnawinge care:

---

²⁶ *both*] "o" *deleted after* "o" *MS*
²⁷ *he gave*] *inserted above with caret*

And whose satietie[28] repentence brings. /
What great deseases and what griping greifs
5   Unto the body pleasures do procure,
As fruit and punishment for life impure?
Whose motions first what sweete delight it hath
I do not knowe, but *he* shall understand,
Who will his passions past againe remember,
10   That sops of sorrow pleasures end doth render.
Who if they can make man full fortunate,
No cause why beasts should not be happie thought,
Whose whole intent is bodies lust to fill.
Pleasure of wife and children honest is,
15   Yet is it said somewhat unnaturall,
Y[t] some as torments have their children found.
Wherof how gnawinge is mans whole estate
I neede not showe to you, who proved have
The same, and who remaine in hevines.
20   Where in the speach of my *Euripides*
    I do allow, who thought it happie *state*,
    By childrens want to be unfortunate.

Meter · 7 ·

Vaine pleasures all in generall
   These harmes do bring,
Who them enioy, they him anoy
   Much like bees stinge. /

5   *Pleasure doth fly so sone as she*
   Hath hony left:
With sowrest smart, peircinge mans hart
   Of ioy bereft.

Prose · 8 · /

Wherefore no doubt but to[29] *beatitude*
These foresaid waies are pathes erroneous,[30]
Nor these can bringe you whither they make showe

---

[28] satietie] felicitie *deleted with* satietie *inserted above*
[29] to] be *deleted after* to MS
[30] erroneous] "o" *inserted above with caret after* "e"

But now I will most breiflie demonstrate
5 Wth what enormities they wrapped are.
ffor what? To heape up riches will you[31] strive?
But you must take it from the owner then.
Would you excell in noble dignities?
But you must bowe unto the giver then.
10 And who so will excell in hono[urs] place
By begginge of the same becometh base.
Would you wish might? Subiect to vile deceipts
And treacheries of *Subiects* thine thou art.   25 [r]
Require you *glory*?[32] But by great attempts
15 Distracted, you to live secure shall cease. /
Would you yo[ur] daies in pleasure spend secure?
But who will not disdaine and cast away
His bodies service vilest lump of clay.
Concerning such who bodies *goodes* prefer,
20 Of slender and of fraile estate they boast.
For *Elephantes* in stature, *Bulls* in strength,
Tygers in swiftnes can you overmatch?
Behould the *heavenes hugenes* fixed frame
And swift celeritie, then cease at length
25 Terrestriall abiect things so to admire. /
Heavens externall *beauty* not so much
Deserveth admiration, as in y^t
By reasons rule directed firme they are.
Brightnes of beauty passeth swift awaye
30 More fugitive then are the fragrant flowers.
But if so be (as *Aristotle* saith)
Mens eies were sharpe, as *Lynces* eies, to peirce
Into all obiects, would not seemely shape
Of *Alcibiades* his outward showe,
35 Percinge into his entralls, foule appeare?
Wherefore not *nature*, but mans eies defect
To cause, whie man doth seeme so beautifull. /
Well, well, yo[ur] bodies *goodes* of price esteeme.
Yet knowe y^t tertian ague° can dissolve
40 Blossomes of beauty wch you much admire. /

---

[31] you] seeke *deleted after* you *MS*
[32] glory?] Subiect *deleted after* glory? *MS*

Of all wch things I may in breife conclude,
That these wch yeild no *good* as they do seeme
Nor perfect are by iust concourse of *goodes*,
    They neither serve as pathes to happie state:
45   Nor are a force to make you fortunate. /

Meter 8 · /

Alas how ignorance doth sely° man seduce!
No gould you seek from trees, nor gemmes from vines you crave,
Your nets on hills you cast not fish thence to produce,
*Nor on the Tyrrhen Sea you seeke not goates to have.*³³
5   *The gredy gulphes in serginge Seas mankind hath found,*
*Also what streames with pearle, or fish for purple*³⁴ *flow:*
Where tender fish for meate, or Echins° sharpe abound,
But where true good consisteth wch you seeke to know,
You blinded men are furthest of to see and find,
10   *Who search under the earth, for that wch raignes in skies.*
What shall I wish beseeminge such a folish mynd,
But this, let them hunt after wealth, and dignities,
    And after that false goods they prove wth trial sowre,
    Then may they understand true goods unfained power. / [25 v]

Prose 9 · /

Thus farr to have depainted forth the forme
As false felicitie, this may suffice.
Markinge my method, wch if you behould
True good I must by order now unfould. /
5   *B.* I see, said I, wee neith[er] can obtain
By *wealth, abundance,* nor by *Kingdoms might*:
Nor *honour,* by *highe* place, nor true *renowne*
By *fame* wee gaine, nor ioy, by vaine *delight.* /
P. Do you the cause hereof not understand?
10   *B*: I seeme as in a glasse these things to knowe. /
P: Doubtles the reason is in readines.
For what is simple and in *nature* one,
Error of men the same doth separate,
Transferringe it from true and perfect *good*

---

³³ *have] over-written in dark ink*
³⁴ *purple] "r" inserted above with caret*

15   To seeming *showes*, and to imperfect things.
        Dost thou suppose yᵗ what doth nothinge want
        Is void of powerfull might? *Bo*: No sure, said I.
        P. Rightlie thou saiest, for if yᵗ any thinge
        Be weake in force, it needeth elswher ayde. /
20   *B*: Its true, said I. *P.* Then is the *nature* one
        Of wealth sufficience and princelie power. /
        B: It seemeth so. *P.* And dost thou thinke such state
        Unworthie is, or rath[er] worthie most
        To be esteemed cheife in reverence.
25   *B*: The dignitie therof wee must confess.
        P. Then let us add moreover *Reverence*
        To this sufficiens and princely power
        That all as one wee may account these three.
        B: Wee must if to the truth wee will agree.
30   *Ph*: What then, said *shee*, do you esteeme this base
        Or els to be a thinge most glorious?
        But marke what you have granted not to want,
        And to be most of might and worthiest
        Of *honours highe*, you may not yᵗ deprive
35   Of *glories* crowne, as though it had defect,
        Or yᵗ in any sort it were abiect. /
        B: I cannot but confesse the same to be
        Most glorious. *P.* Then must wee needs confesse
        Glory to be all one wᵗʰ th'oth[er] three.
40   *B*: That followeth well, said I. *P*: Then must you grant
        Yᵗ what requireth no externall ayde,
        Wᶜʰ is of might all things to bringe to passe,
        Wᶜʰ is renowned and most reverend
        The same to rest in ioyfull pleasant state.
45   *B*: I cannot see how unto such a good   26 ·[r]
        Anguish at all can any way ascend.
        Then sith yo[ur] former proufs appeared plaine,
        In ioyfullnes the same must needs remaine. /
        P. And this will follow also from those proufs
50   That names of *Plenty, might renowned fame*
        Honour and pleasure are distinguished:
        But yet in substance these do all agree.
        B: Most true, said I. *P.* This therefore, wᶜʰ is one
        By *nature* simple, humaine ignorance

55   Devided hath, and whilst he would inioy
          A part of y^t wch cannot parted stand,
          Man neith[er] doth inioy therof a part
          Nor hath the whole from whom he doth depart. /
          B: Wherin said I do men true *good* devide?
60   P. Who so requireth wealth, said *she*, his want
          For to abandon aymeth not at power,
          But wisheth rath[er] to remaine obscure
          Who also many pleasures naturall
          W^{th}draweth lest the wealth he got he lose.
65   Hereby he cannot gaine sufficience
          Who wanteth *might*, whom grevances do vex,
          Whom basenes and obscuritie doth hide.
          Now he y^t *might* only in price doth hould
          Riches doth spend, and pleasure doth despice,
70   Nor *honour* wantinge *might*, nor *fame* doth weighe,
          But yet how many helpes him faile you see.
          For oft he necessaries so much wants
          Y^t he wth cares is crossed manifould
          W^{ch} when *he* cannot from his hart expell
75   Of *might* he is deprived by y^t meanes.
          W^{ch} he above all things esteemed most.
          Concerning *honours*, *glory*, and *delight*,
          In argument the same we may conclude.
          For whereas these are one, whoso some one
80   Of these alone w^{th}out the rest requireth
          Obtayneth not y^t one wch he desireth.[35]
          B. What then, said I? P. Yf any man to have
          These alltogither doth at once desire
          The supreame *good* he wisheth to inioy
85   But can he find the same in these vaine showes
          Whom I demonstrate not to be of force
          For to effect what they do promise men.
          B. No by no meanes, said I. P. Therfore in these
          W^{ch} seeme one only part of happines
90   For to afford, we may not goe about
          Beatitude to find. B. This thing I grant   [26 v]
          And nothinge can, then this, more true be spoke.

---

[35] desireth] "o" *deleted after* "i" *MS*

P. The forme, said *she*, of seeming happines
And causes also of the same you heare:
95   Now turn thy sight of mynd contrariwise
True happines wch I thee promised
To teach, thou also shalt now understand.
B: This thinge, said I, the blind may clearely see
And you the same before declared have
100   Wher you the seeminge causes pointed at. /
For y^t is true and perfect happines,
(Unles I be deceived) wch doth make
A man sufficient in him selfe to be,
Mighty, and reverend, and glorious,
105   And wth *sweete pleasures ioy* replenished.
And y^t you may perceive I these things marke
Attentivelie in *mynd* I understand
That what can any one of these afford,
Because these all are one, the same must be
110   Wthout all doubt *compleate felicitie.*
P. O foster child happie herein thou art
Yf hereunto one thinge annexed be.
B. What thinge, said I? *P*. Wheth[er] do you suppose
In mortall and frayle things is any state
115   Y^t may to such *beatitude* aspire.
B: No verilie I thinke and this is plaine
Proved by you y^t more to add were vaine.
P. The *Image* of *true good* unto mankind
Or els *imperfect good* these seeme to yeild,
120   But true and perfect *goodnes* cannot give. /
B: This thing I graunt, said I, wth full assent.
P. Then for so much as you have understood
What true *good* is and what *beatitude*
Doth counterfeite, it doth remaine y^t you
125   Now understand the way and meanes whereby
You may true *happines* attaine unto.
B: This is the thinge wch I most ardentlie
Have longe expected to be by you taught.
P. But sith (as *Plato in Timæo* saith)
130   In smallest things *Gods ayde* we must implore
What thinke you fittest herein to be done
That we to finde the seate of supreame *good*

May worthie be. *B*: Wee ought to invocate
The father of all things, whom if wee passe
135   Then no begining can be founded stronge
Ph: Well said, quoth *she*, and therew^th all *she* singe. /

Meter 9 · /   27 ·[r]

O thou who governest the world wth endles reason,
Who art creator of the earth and azur'd skie,
Who dost commande tymes motions to succeede in season,
Who art immoveable yet movest all from highe:
5   *Whom no externall causes could constraine to try*
        The worke of worldes creation first to undertake,
        But thy internall goodnes love the same did make.

All thinges thou dost ordaine like supreme paterns frame
Worldes seemely shape in mynd thou beautifull didst lay,
10   *Creatinge it in Image like unto the same,*
Perfect all parts commaundinge constantly to stay.
Thou Elements proportions measuringe dost waighe,
        That cold with heate and dry with moist keepe harmony,
        Lest heavy earth descend, or fire should mount more highe.

15   *Heavens Intelligence thou in the middle knittinge,*
Containinge triple nature, movinge all below
Thou dost resolve, directinge it by sphæres befittinge,
Who when two^36 waies his motions seperated goe,
Againe it moveth inwardly itself to knowe,
20   *And searcheth out thy hidden nature most profound,*
        And with like understandinge moveth heavens rounde. /

Immortall soules of men alike didst create,
And thinges inferior their life from thee they have:
Who placinge soules of men in earth and heavens state,
25   *In mercy callinge them to thee thou dost them save,*
By thy abundant love, which to all essence gave. /
        O father graunt our mindes may now ascend to thee,
        Fountaine of supreme good vouchsafe wee cleare may see. /

---

^36 *two*] *tow* MS

Vouchsafe when light by us is found embrace wee maye
30 *With evident myndes sight at large thy goodnes deare:*
Disperse the clustred cloudes and drosse of earthly clay,
And us with light illuminate, for thou art cleare.
Tranquillity to good men thou dost cause t'apeare,
      Who art the end, begininge, director, and guide,
35   *Our Captaine, and our path, our home, where we should byde. /*

Prose 10 /

Because of *good imperfect*, and the forme
Of perfect good, thou hast before beheld,
Now must I shewe wherein this p[er]fect state
Of right beatitude consists, I iudge,
5   And first herein I ought to search, I thinke,
Whether such good as you defined have
In *nature* may be founde, lest *shadowes* vaine   [27 v]
From truth therof o[ur] daizeled mynds detaine.
That such good is existent no man doubts
10 And that it is of all *good* things the springe. /
For what imperfect named is, is said
To be imperfect in regard it doth
From y^t wch hath perfection disagree. /
From whence it is y^t if in any find
15 Imperfect any thinge shall seeme to be,
In y^t kind perfect somethinge needs must be.
For take away perfection who can see
Imperfectnes in any kind to be?
ffor *nature* neither did begininge take
20 From things of weakest worth unfinished,
But *shee* procedinge from things absolute
Unto these last and weakest works declines.
Now if, as I before declared have,
Felicitie imperfect in things fraile
25 Consisteth, then it seemeth questionles
There also is a perfect happines. /
B: Most true, said I, these reasons yo[urs] conclude.
P. Now where this good remayneth gather thus:
That *God* of all things is the *sovereigne good*
30 Common consent of all men doth approve.
For sith then *God* noe better thinge maye be

Who doubteth that is *good* y^t passeth all.
Now reason verifies *God* to be *good*,
Y^t perfect state of *good* in him doth rest.
35   For otherwise he were not cheife of all.
For perfect *good* elswhere more excellent,
And far more aunctient then he would seeme.
ffor all things perfect extant were before
Imperfect things. Wherefore lest reason should
40   Wthout fitt obiect infinit extend
That *supreme God* wth *perfect supreme good*
Is most replenished we must confesse.
Now perfect *good* is *true beatitude*,
In supreme *God* therefore it must consist. /
45   *B*: This thinge I understande, said I, nor cause
To contradict these principles I see.
P. But marke I praie you how religiouslie
And soundly you can prove that *highest God*
Doth most of all abound wth *highest good*. /
50   *Bo*: How is this prov'd?³⁷ said I. *Ph*: Do not suppose
This father of all things received hath
This cheifest *good* wherewth he doth abound
From any cause externall, or to have
The same in nature as a bare possession
55   In substance dive^{rs} from his *deitie*³⁸: 28 [r]
For if you iudge it came from other meanes,
That thing wch gave it were more excellent
Then y^t wch needed to receive the same. /
But not wthout greate reason wee confesse,
60   All things to *God* give place in worthines. /
Now if by *nature* this in him consist,
But yet by reason is distinguished:
When as wee speake of what is sovereigne,
Let man imagine who in one hath linckt
65   These two wch are by *nature* things distinct. /
Lastlie, what thinge is dive^{rs} from the rest,
It is not y^t from wch it dive^{rs} is:
Wherefore what thinge by *nature* is distinct,

---

³⁷ prov'd] "e" *deleted after* "v" *with apostrophe inserted above*
³⁸ deitie] ei *over-written in dark ink*

From cheifest good, cheif good that cannot be.³⁹

70   W^{ch} to impute to *God* most heynous were,
        More excellent then whom it may appeare?
        ffor doubtles nothinge may more worthie be
        By *natures* force, then his begininge was:
        Wherefore, what is *originall* of all,

75   I may conclude in essence it must be
        The supreme *good. B.* And not unworthily.⁴⁰
        P. But supreme *good* (you graunt) is *happines.*
        B. I grant it is. *P.* Then must you also grant
        Y^t *good alone is cheif felicitie.*

80   *B.* Yo[ur] p[re]misses I cannot well deny
        Whose consequence most plaine produced is.
        P. Marke well how hence, more firmly this I prove:
        Y^t two cheif *goodes* wch are distinguished
        Cannot togither stand. For sure it is

85   Distinct *good* things cannot be all as one:
        And therefore neither can be absolute:
        Sith one is wantinge to supplie the rest.
        Now it is certaine what imperfect is
        Cannot be said to be the supreme *good.* /

90   Then in no wise those good things dive^{rs} are
        W^{ch} are supreme. But I have shew'd before
        Felicitie and God are cheifest *good*:
        Wherfore all one coheareth *cheife felicitie*
        In essens wth the *eternall diety.*

95   *B.* Nothinge more true, or more in reason sound,
        Or more beseeminge *God*, we may conclude.
        P. Moreover as *Geometricians* use
        In demonstrac[i]on of theire principles
        Some consequence from thence for to infer,

100   A *corollarie* so will I thee give. /
        Because men be by gaininge *happines*
        Blessed, and blessednes is very *deity*,
        By gettinge godlines we blessed be. /
        Now as by gaininge iustice, men are iust,   [28 v]

---

³⁹ From cheifest ... cannot be] *interlineated*
⁴⁰ unworthily] un *inserted above with caret*

105   By havinge wisdome men are counted wise
       So gaininge *godlines* doth make men *Gods.*
       Then every blessed man[41] is as a *God*
       For thoughe by *nature God* but one can be,
       Yet many may pertake the *deitie.*
110   *Bo:* Whether a consequent or *corollarie*
       You call this speach it is most p[re]cious.
       P. Yea nothinge can more worthie be then this
       W^ch reason biddeth hereunto to ioyne.
       B. What is that thinge? *P.* Sith blessednes consists
115   Of many things, wheth[er] all these concurre
       Into one bodie of *beatitude,*
       Into their certaine parts distinguished?
       Or wheth[er] any one of them performe
       The solid[42] substance of *felicitie,*
120   Whereto all oth[er] things referred be.
       B: I wish you would this thinge declare at large.
       P. Do not wee count *beatitude* a good?
       B: Yes supreme *good. P:* You must hereto this add,
       Beatitude is cheife sufficiency.
125   It also is cheife *might, and honour* cheife,
       Glory, and pleasure cheife it is. *B.* What then?
       P.[43] Are all these *goodes,* sufficiencie, and *might,*
       W^th all the rest, members of blessed state?
       Or are theie all (as to theire highest heade)
130   Referred to cheife good? *B.* I understand
       What you discussinge, for to prove intend,
       But I desire hereof to heare yo[ur] end. /
       P.[44] The difference hereof thus understand
       Members of *happines* if all these were
135   One from the oth[er] then they differ would
       For this the *nature true* of members is,
       Diverse coheare one body for to make.
       B. But these are proved all as one to be.
       P. Therefore they are not parts thereof: for so

---

[41] man] name *altered to* man *(initial* "n" *changed to* "m" *with final* "e" *deleted)*
[42] solid] "l" *inserted above with caret*
[43] P.] *inserted in left margin*
[44] P.] B. MS

140   Of only member one, *felicity*
       Should seeme for to consist, wch may not be.
       Bo:[45] Noe doubt thereof but I the rest expect.
       Ph: All other things to *good* referred are
       For men require sufficiency because
145   It seemeth good, and men wish puissaunce
       Because the same in like sort seemeth *good*,
       Concerninge *honour*, *glory*, and *delight*,
       The same wee maye conclude. ffor only good
       Of mans desire is finall cause and drifte. /
150   ffor what in truth, nor in the *show* of truth
       Seemeth no native *goodnes* to retaine,
       Such thinge is not required. Otherwise   29 [r]
       What things by *nature* are not *good* indeede,
       Yet if they seeme to beare a shew of *good*,
155   As if they were true *good*, they wished are. /
       From whence it is the summe and finall end
       Of mens desires to *goodnes* seemes to tend. /
       Now for what cause another thinge is sought
       The cause it selfe seemes to be wished most:
160   As if a man will ride because of health,
       He doth not seeke so much y^t exercise
       Of rydinge, as he doth th'effect of health.
       Wherefore sith all things for the cause of *good*[46]
       Are sought the same are not so much desired[47]
165   Of *men*, as is the very *good* it selfe.
       But for what thinge all oth[ers] wished are
       We granted have to be *felicity*.
       Wherefore *felicity* is only sought.
       ffrom whence it is y^t *good* and happie state
170   *One only substance*[48] do participate. /
       B. No cause to contradict yo[ur] former speach
       I can p[er]ceive. *P.* But *God* and blessednes
       All one to be I have made manifest.
       B. You have indeede. *P.* Then safe I may conclude

---

[45] *Bo:*] *inserted in left margin*
[46] *good*] *health deleted with good inserted above with caret*
[47] desired] *"o" deleted after "i" MS*
[48] *substance*] *"b" inserted above with caret*

175   In perfect *good Gods essence* doth abyde
And not in any other thinge beside. /

Meter 10 /

Drawe neare ye mortall men blindly deceaved,
Whom vaine delights in cursed chaines have bound:
Obscuringe much your myndes of truth bereaved,
Here quiet rest from all your toyles is found,

5   *Here haven calme of pleasant peace remaineth,*
       Here is the Refuge which your woes sustaineth. /

What Tagus yeildeth with his goulden sand,
Or river Hermus with his glitteringe shoare,
Or Indus run[n]inge neare the scorchinge land,
10   *Grene perles and whit wch hath aboundant store,*
       Cannot illuminate your sight of mynd,
       But rather wrappeth you in Error blinde. /

These thinges which folish myndes so much delight,
Do issue from the caves of basest ground:
15   *Brightnes wherewith heaven is ruled right*
Expelleth darknes, wch your myndes hath drown'd:
       Who clearely can conceive this worthy light,
       Will not esteme the bemes of Phœbus bright.

Prose 11 ·   [29 v]

B. Hereto I give consent, sith all o[ur] proufs
By soundest demonstrac[i]ons lincked are.
P. Of what account will you this thing esteeme
Yf what this *goodnes* is you understand?
5   B. Of infinit account, for therewthall
God who is *supreme good* I shall conceive.
P. This thinge by reason sound I will make plaine,
But let in mynd my former proufs remaine. /
B. I them observe. P. Have not I shewed thee
10 Y^t those things wch of most men wished are
Are for this cause not *true nor perfect goodes,*
In y^t amongst them selves repugnance is.
And sith to one the other wanting is,
Full good and absolute they cannot yeild.

15   Theie only then *true perfect good* become
        When into[49] one theire forme and force is tyed
        And what sufficiens is, the[50] same should be
        Might, honour, worthy fame, and *sweete delight*.
        All wch unles in one they do agree,
20   No reason why they should required be.
        B: These things declared are before, wherin
        No doubt doth rest. *P.* Then what things are not *good*
        When as they parted are, but beinge one
        Good things become, doth not such *good* arise
25   Because they are united all in one?
        B: It seemeth so. *P.* But will you graunt, or us,
        Y^t what is *good* receaveth all his worth
        By takinge part of *highest good*? *B.* I graunt.
        P. Then in[51] like sort this must you also grant,
30   Y^t *unity and good* agree in one,
        For all *one* essence such things do containe,
        Whose *naturall effects* all one remaine. /
        B. I cannot this deny. *P.* Do you not know
        Y^t every beinge doth so longe persist
35   As it is one: but is dissolved then,
        When *unity* it leaveth? *B.* In what sort?
        Ph: Like as when soule and body do concurre
        In livinge creatures all in *nature* one,
        The same a livinge creature named is. /
40   But when this unitie dissolved is
        By seperac[i]on of the parts asunder,
        It vanisheth and is no more that[52] creature. /
        Mans bodie likewise when it doth persist
        By ioyned members in conformitie,
45   So longe appeareth perfect humaine shape:
        But if the bodies parts distracted be,
        It ceaseth to continue as[53] it was.   30·/[r]
        In like sort whoso veiweth all things els,

---

[49] into] *word deleted after* into *MS*
[50] same] *word deleted after* same *MS*
[51] in] *inserted above with caret*
[52] that] "a" *deleted with* that *inserted above with caret*
[53] as] *word deleted with* as *inserted above*

Shall plaine perceive, y^t things so longe endure,
50   While one they are, but when theire *unity*
Dissolved is, they longer cease to be. /
B. Perusinge many things I cannot see
But y^t yo[ur] words containe a certaine truth.
P. Doth any thinge by *naturall* instinct,
55   Leavinge the love of beinge, ever wish
His owne distruction, and corruption?
B. Yf I consider creatures wch inioy
An appetite to chose and to refuse:
None can I finde, unles by outward meanes
60   They be constrained, wch to live refuse,
And willinglie incline unto theire end.
ffor every creature to p[re]serve his health
Endeavoureth but dreadfull death they flie. /
For hearbes and trees and creatures wantting life,
65   What to conclude, my mynd doth rest in doubt. /
Ph: Surely no cause herein to doubt you have[54]
Sith hearbes and trees you may observe to grow
In places wth theire *nature* best agreinge.
Where, so much as theire *nature* will permit,
70   They neither may decay nor[55] come to end. /
ffor some in fields, and some on *Mountaines* growe,
Some live in *marish grounds*, some cleave to *Rocks*,
The barren sands yeild some, wch if you seeke
Elswhere to plant, they with[er] straight, and dy. /
75   But *nature* needefull things to all doth give,
Who doth endeavoure that they perish not.
What shall I say, y^t all these sucke theire foode
By *Rootes*, as if theire mouthes were hid in earth[56]
And by theire pith their strength and rinde disperce. /
80   Further the softest part, namely the pith
In inner parts contayned all waies is,
Inclosed round wth solid parts of wood. /
Lastlie the *rynde* against the rage of ayre
Opposed is, all sturdie stormes to beare. /

---

[54] *Ph*: Surely ... have] *inserted above*
[55] nor] or *MS*
[56] earth] ground *deleted with* earth *inserted in right margin*

85   ffurther how great is *natures* diligence
        All things to propagate by *meanes* of seede,
        W^{ch} doth not only for a tyme remaine,
        But still producinge new, like *engines* fast
        Who knoweth not y^t *species* ever last. /
90   Those creatures allso wanting sence and life
        Do not they likewise *natures aide require.* /
        For why doth *lightnes* cause the fire to mount,
        Or why doth *weight* drawe downward still the earth
        But y^t such place and motions are most fitt.
95   Moreover what is most convenient   [30 v]
        By *nature* every thinge doth y^t retaine,
        But contraries wch doth corrupt refraine. /
        Hard things, as stones, wth solid parts cohere,
        W^{ch} will not easely dissolved be.
100   But *liquid thinges, as*[57] *aire and water are,*
        Wth ease you may devide, yet these returne
        United streight[58] togith[er] wth theire parts. /
        But noe partic[i]on doth the fire admit. /
        I do not of such motions now intreate
105   As come from will of understanding mynd,
        But touchinge naturall intention
        As when received foode we do concocte
        Not thinking thereuppon: That in o[ur] sleepe
        Wee draw o[ur] breath not knowing by what meanes:
110   For appetite in creatures to persist
        Proceedeth not from any will of mynd,
        But *nature* causeth it by course of kinde. /
        ffor oft externall causes, do constraine
        The will to yeild to dy, w^{ch} *nature* feares. /
115   Againe y^t act of generation
        Wherby alone creatures continued are
        Nature requireth, but will doth restraine.
        So this desire to be doth not proceede
        From creatures moc[i]on, but from *Natures* deede. /
120   For *divine providence* vouchsafed hath
        To creatures all this meanes still to endure,

---

[57] *as*] *inserted above with caret*
[58] streight] "h" *deleted after second* "t" *MS*

Y^t so much as they can they seek to live.
No reason then you have to stand in doubt
Y^t creatures all by *naturall* instinct
125 Still permanent their state for to defend
Entirely wish, and to avoide their end. /
B. I grant y^t now I certainely conceive,
What seemed late my *iudgement* to deceive.
P. Now what desireth to continue still
130 Y^t thinge requireth to be only one,
W^{ch} *unity* dissolved, you dissolve
The *essens* of the thing it selfe. B. It's true.
P. All things therefore wish to be one. B.^{59} I graunt.
P.^{60} But y^t, *that one is good* I proved. B. Yea.
135 P. Wherefore all things require what thing is good
W^{ch} not unaptlie you may well describe,
That, *that is good* wch wished is of all. /
B. More certaine nothing can be searched out. /
For eyther all to nothing are referred,
140 Wanting theire head straying wthout a *guide*:
Or if such thinge their be wch all things wish,
The sovereigne *good* of all the same must be.   31 ·[r]
P. O *foster child* exceedinglie I ioy
Sith certaine truth in mynd thou fixed hast. /
145 For in this thinge^{61} to thee y^t doth appeare
W^{ch} thou hast said thou didst not understand. /
B. What thinge is y^t? P. Of all things what might be
The finall end, wch certainely is that
W^{ch} of all creatures is desired most.
150 The wch because I proved to be good,
Wee must acknowledge y^t the finall end
Of creatures all, to *goodnes cheife* doth tend.^{62} /

Meter 11 · /
Who doth with study longe the truth inquire,
And with no Errors wisheth to be moved,

---

^{59} B.] *inserted above with caret*
^{60} P.] *inserted in left margin*
^{61} thinge] *word deleted after* thinge
^{62} tend] *word (possibly* bend*) altered to* tend

Must in him selfe his reasons light retyre
Discoursinge[63] longe untill the right be proved:
5   What he intendeth let his mynd desire
To keepe in store of memory approved.
　　So cloudes of Error chased from his mynd,
　　More light than Phœbus yeildeth, he shall finde.

For men are not deprived whole of light,
10   Thoughe drossie earth oblivious lumpe they beare:
But certaine seedes of truth inhere in sight,
W^{ch} exercise in Arts doth cause t'appeare.
For how could children asked answere right,
Unles in mynd the seede of truth theire were?
15   　　And if[64] the Muse of Plato soundeth true,
　　What men do learne their mynd doth but renew.

Prose 12 · /
To Plato willinglie I give consent. /
For these things I to mynd againe recall,
My mynd oppressed first wth earthlie drosse
And after wth the cloge of gnawinge greife,
5   I lost thereby the knowledge of this thinge. /
P. Yf you my former Arguments respect,
No longer can y^t thinge from you be hid,
But you shall call to mynd what you before
Acknowledged you did not understand.
10   B. What thinge is y^t? Ph: Wherby the world is rul'd.
B: That I myne ignorance acknowledged
I do remember wch allthoughe I knowe
I wish you would the same more plainely show.
P. You doubted not before but y^t this world
15   By God is governed. B. Nor yet I thinke
Or ever shall y^t this I ought to doubt   [31 v]
And wth what reasons moved I suppose
That this is true breiflie I will disclose.
This world consistinge[65] of such dive^{rs} parts,

---

[63] Discoursinge] "r" inserted above with caret
[64] if] inserted above with caret
[65] consistinge] eth deleted after "t" with inge inserted above with caret

20   And contraries, had not conioyn'd in one,
      Unles theire had been one, who could unite
      Such divers parts: wch parts though they were knit,
      Yet the *diversitie of natures* force
      Repugnant still would have distracted all,
25   Unles theire had been *one* who could containe
      What he united constant to remain.
      Nor *natures order* could so sure proceede,
      Neither such constant motions could performe
      Distinct in place, in tyme, in might, in space,
30   In qualities, unles there had been one
      Who could these *manifould varieties*
      Of change unchangeable him selfe dispose.
      This who doth guide and move the creatures all,
      By usuall phrase of speach him, *God*, I call.
35   *P.* Because these things you fully understand
      Small labo[ur] now remayneth to restore
      Yo[ur] *mynd* yo[ur] *native* cuntry safe to see,
      And to behould the state of *blessednes*.
      But let us not from purpose o[urs] digresse. /
40   Did not wee count *sufficiency* to rest
      In blessednes? And did not wee agree
      That *God* is verie *blessednes?* *B.* Yea sure. /
      P. Then to direct the world no outward ayde
      He wanteth otherwise if^{66} he should want
45   *Perfect sufficiencie* he could not have.
      B. This reason is of force. *P.* Then by him selfe
      Alone he ruleth all. *B.* No doubt hereof.
      P. Now *God* is proved to be finall *good.*
      B. I well remember it. *P.* By *goodnes* then
50   All things he doth dispose: sith of him selfe
      He ruleth all, whom to be *good* we grant.
      This is the sterne and only helme whereby
      The world doth stable stand and incorrupt. /
      B. Most willinglie hereto I give assent,
55   For in some measure I did this foresee
      Before perceivinge what you would conclude. /
      P. I thinke the same, for now as I suppose

---

^{66} if] *inserted above with caret*

More vigilent for to conceive the truth
Yo[ur] eies you frame. But now what I will speake
60   Is nothinge less apparent. *B.* What is y^t?
P. Sith *God* is said iustly all things to guide
W^th *helme* of *goodnes*: and sith creatures all
As I have taught by *naturall instinct*
Aime at this *good*, no doubt but willinglie   32·/[r]
65   They yeild to be disposed at his will. /
And freely frame them selves to his com[m]and,
As instruments convenient and fitt
Squared for their *Disposers regiment.*
B. It must be so, for *happie Regiment*
70   It would not seeme, if such a slavish *yoke*
It were, as creatures would resist to beare
And not their safety, who sustaine the same. /
P. Then nothinge wch observeth *natures lawe*
Attempteth *God* to contradict? *B.* Nothinge.
75   *P.* If any should attempt him to resist
Could they p[re]vaile against him whom wee graunt
To be most *mighty in beatitude?*
B. Prevaile they cannot. *P.* Therefore nothing will
Or can resist this *supreme God?*[67] *B.* No sure.
80   *P.* Then y^t is *cheifest good*, wch all w^th *might*
Doth rule, and wth his *goodnes* doth dispose.
B. Oh how not only yo[ur] collections
Of reasons sound, but also these yo[ur] words
My *mind* delight! Ashamed now I am
85   To see my folly breathinge blasphemies. /
P. In fables you have heard[68] y^t *Giants* erst
Attempted to encounter wth the skies,
But by the *fortitude of God benigne*,
Meete for their merits they deposed were.
90   But let us now conferr o[ur] arguments
Perhaps by such conflict some worthie sparke
Of truth will shine. *B.* Use yo[ur] discretion.
P. That *God allmighty* is, no man will doubt.
B. No man, unles he be not well in mynd. /

---

[67] *God*] "o" *deleted after* "o" *MS*
[68] heard] hard *MS*

95   *Ph.* But who *Allmighty* is, nothing can bee,
        W^{ch} he cannot effect. *B.* Not anythinge.
        P. Now can this *God* performe things evill. *B.* No.
        P. Then evill nothinge is, sith he cannot effect
        The same, whose *might* is voide of all defect.
100   *B.* Do you delude me, framinge for my steps
        An endles laborinth wherin sometyme
        Where you should enter out, you enter in,
        Againe where you should enter in, you seeme
        For to stepe out? Of *Gods* simplicitie
105   Will you compile such reasons circuler?
        For late begininge wth *beatitude*
        You proved it to be the *highest good*,
        W^{ch} you affirmed to consist in *God.* /
        Againe you proved *God cheife good* to be
110   And perfect *happines*, from whence no man
        Blessed to be but he should be a *God*
        By needefull consequent you did inferre.   [32 v]
        Againe you said the forme of *goodnes* was
        Essence of God, and of beatitude. /
115   W^{ch} *unity* you said was that same *good*
        W^{ch} by all creatures was desired most. /
        That *God* by *goodnes reines* all things doth rule
        You likewise did conclude. And y^t all things
        Wth willinge service did obey his will.
120   Lastlie that *vice in nature* nothing is. /
        And these you proved not wth principles
        Externall, but inherent in themselves.
        One to the other yeilding ornaments
        Of credit wth familiar *arguments.*
125   *P.* I do not dally but by *divine ayde*,
        Whom late in praier I sollicited,
        The deepest *mistery* I passed have.
        For such the form of *divine essence* is
        Y^t things externall cannot it conceive,
130   Nor any outward thinge it will receive. /
        But as *Parmenides* therof doth say
        Things manifould thou by thine owne accord
        Reducinge to their circles dost unite.
        That is the movinge orbe of things he swaies

135   But doth him selfe im[m]ovable conserve.
           Yf forraine reasons I did not alledge,
           But such as were wthin the bounds of y^t
           Wherof we did entreate, no cause you have
           To wonder, sith as *Plato* hath you taught,
               Our words wth matter lincked ought t'agree,
140   In perfect leauge of neare affinitie. /

                        Meter 12 · /
           Happie is he, cleare springe who can behould
               Of goodnes cheife. /
           Happie is he from clogge of earthly mould[69]
               Who findes releife. /
5   *Orpheus death of his wyfe bewaylinge late*
               With wofull cries,
           When woodes to move his songe did penetrate
               In stranges wise. /
           When streames to stand his swetest harpe did bynd
10   *His notes to heare:*
           With lions feirce when he did lincke the hinde,
               Voide of all feare.
           When hare was not afraide the dogge to see
               Rapt with his songe,
15   *When loyall love in Orpheus inwardly*
               Had boyled long. /   33 [r]
           Those plesant notes then could not him[70] *asswage*
               Who all thinges tam'd
           But that to hell he went, the Gods in rage
20   *As cruel blamed. /*
           Where tuninge sonnets sweete on soundinge stringes
               He playeth still,
           What songes he sucked from the sweetest springes
               Of Muses skill. /
25   *Waylinge so much as teares would him permit*
               And loyall love,
           Th'Infernall spirits, his wife for to remit,
               He seekes to move.

---

[69] *mould*] clay *deleted with* mould *inserted in right margin*
[70] *him*] *inserted above with caret*

The Porter Cerberus admyringe standes
30   *Strange notes to heare,*
The furies which wth hot revenginge brandes
       The wicked feare.
Now mourninge flow with teares, nor Ixions wheele
       Doth now torment,
35   *The thirst wch Tantalus was wonte to feele*
       Doth now relent.
The vultur doth not Titius liver eate.
       Th'infernall Kinge
With pity moved, said, cease to intreate
40   *We grant this thinge*
Thy wife bought with thy melody receave,
       Yet this provide,
For her you looke not back, till Hell you leave
       Lest back she slyde. /
45   *But who by lawes can lovers harts constraine*
       To stand in awe?
Unfained love doth in it selfe containe
       A greater lawe.
Orpheus, alas, now redy to depart
50   *From hellish crue,*
Turninge to see Euridice his hart
       Her lost and slue. /
This fable doth respect them who intend
       To frame their mynd
55   *To gaine the supreme good, for who descend*
       With senses blinde
Into th'infernall lake, are overcome
       And loose also
What guiftes celestial they before have won
60   *Who thither goe. /*
       Finis Libri terty · /

The Physick[1] of Philosophie, compiled
by Anicius Manlius Torquatus Severinus
Boethius, touchinge the
consolation of Lady
Philosophie, in the
tyme of his exile. /

The fourth booke: wherin she partly purgeth
his errors, touching Gods providence, and partly
comforteth him with cordiall receipts. /

The first prose ·

These things when as *Lady Philosophie*,
Wth gravity of seemely countenance,
Myldly and sweetlie had in verses songe:
Then I not fullie yet ingrafted greife
5   Having forgot her speech did interrupt.
B: O you *Reveyler of true light*, said I,
Yo[ur] fluent speech wch hitherto you use,
Both[2] for the divine speculac[i]on
Thereof, as also by yo[ur] reasons sound,
10   To be invincyble you demonstrat.
And unto me, allthough by pensive greife
For my late wrongs these things forgot I had,
Yet they were not wholely unknowne, you said.
But this of sorrow mind is no small cause:
15   Y^t, wheras of things a *good guide* there is,
Evile at all can in the world have place. /
Or y^t it can escape unpunished.

---

[1] *Physick*] *physick MS*
[2] both] "o" *deleted after* "o" *MS*

W^{ch} only thinge how much we may³ admire,
Consider seriouslie I you require.
20   But hereunto a thinge of greater weight
May be adioyn'd, y^t when as *Wickednes*⁴
Doth dominere, and triumph florishinge:
Vertue not only iust reward doth want,
But also under foote of miscreants
25   Debased, is wth insolence downetrode.
And in the stead of vile impietie
Sustaineth punishment. W^{ch} thinge to be
Wth in the *Kingdome* of so great a *God*,
Who knoweth all, who is omnipotent,
30   And willing *only good,* no⁵ mortall man
Not only can admire sufficientlie,
But also can lament. Then answered *she,*
P. It should indeede astonishment procure,
And be more horrible then *Monsters* all,   34 ·[r]
35   Yf (as you iudge) in th'house⁶ of such a *Lord,*
Whose familie is best in order set,
Base vessels should be had in cheife respect,
And those of price neglected should seeme vile.
But so it is not, for if wee observe
40   The proposic[i]ons concluded late,
By *Gods* assistance, of whose government
Wee here intreate, you plaine shall understand,
Y^t *honest men* are allwaies *men of might*. /
And *evill men* are abiects base and weake. /
45   Neith[er] y^t *vice* unpunished escapes. /
Nor *vertue* doth deserved *guerdon*° want.
That to *good men felicitie* pertaines.
And to the wicked still unhappie fate. /
And many such conclusions you shall knowe,
50   W^{ch}, quite abandoninge the waylinge late,
May thee wth verity corroborate.
And for as much as you have late beheld,

---

³ may] *inserted above with caret*
⁴ *Wickednes*] *erasure in MS over-written*
⁵ no] No *MS*
⁶ th'house] "e" *deleted with apostrophe inserted above*

By demonstrac[i]ons myne, the verie forme
Of true *beatitude*, as also where
55 It doth consist, you apprehended have.
Omittinge all such things as I suppose
Are fitt to be omitted, I will shewe
To thee, the way wch may thee home recall.
And to thy *mynd* I will such wings affix,
60 Wherew^th it may on highe wth ease ascend
So as expellinge perturbac[i]ons vaine:
Safely you may into yo[ur] native land
Returne, I guidinge you as by the hand.

Meter 1 · /

For winges I have wch speede will make,
Able to peirce the stately skies:
Which when my mynd desires to take,
The earth below she doth despice.
5 *She passinge also globe of ayre,*
Leaveth the cloudes of no account,
And fire, wch with the Heavens sphere
Becometh hot, she doth surmount.
Untill to Planets she ascend,
10 *And Phœbus motions doth behould,*
And Souldier Mars doth view in th'end,
And courses all of Saturne cold.
And through the starry firmament,
W^ch doth adorne the obscure night, [34 v]
15 *When she hath therin longe tyme spent*
Leavinge the Poles, she mounts upright,
Till she behould the christall sky,
And also pleasant Paradice,
Where Lord of Lordes reigneth on highe,
20 *Rulinge the world with iust advice. /*
Movinge the sphære, immoveable,
Remaininge Iudge in glitteringe light.
Whither if thou t'ascend be able,
Thou wilt forget earthes base delight. /
25 *And thus wilt say I call to mynd*
This is my native cuntryes soyle:
From whence my offspringe I do finde,

Here will I rest my steps from toyle.
Which if it please you to behould,
30 *Renouncinge earthes darke glomy face:*
Tyrants whom men in reverence hould,
Ther you may see to have no place.

Prose 2 ·

Then I thus said, these things are wonderfull
W^{ch} you me promise, but I nothinge doubt
You are of *might* the same well to effect.
Only I praie you do no tyme protract,
5 But me instruct, whom you attentive^7 made.
P. First then, said *she*, you ought to understand
That *good men* allwaies are wth *might* endued,
And evill *men* are voyd of seeminge strength.
Both wch by mutuall demonstrac[i]on
10 One by the other manifest is made.
For seing opposit are *good and evill*,
Yf *good* be proved to be powerfull,
Weakenes of *evill* may wee thence collect.
Also by *evills imbicillity*,
15 Wee may conclude *goodnes* stabillity. /
But y^t I may, this my assertion
Wth proufs abundantlie, the more confirme:
Both *propositions* handled severall,
Now one, now th'oth[er], I assume to prove.
20 Two^8 things there are wherin every effect
Of humaine actions do consist and stand:
Namely the *will, and power*: of whom if one
Thereof be wanttinge, nothinge can be done. /
For if a will be wantinge to performe,
25 No man doth undertake, save what he will   35 [r]
But if abilitie be not, to do
What wee intend, the *will* is frustrat made.
Wherby it comes to passe yf you p[er]ceive
Any to wish what he cannot obtaine,
30 Y^t such man wanted strength you may be sure,

---

^{7} attentive] *word deleted with* attentive *inserted above with caret*
^{8} Two] Tow *MS*

What thinge his will desired[9] to procure.
B. Doubtles, said I, this consequent is plaine.
P. Now when you see effected what men would,
That he could do it, can you make doubt? B. No.
35   P. Now what a man *can do* theirin he is
To be esteemed stronge. But he is weake
Wherein his will he cannot execute.
B. This I confess said I. P. But do you not
Remember in my former disputac[i]ons
40   It was concluded, y^t all mens intents
Allthough at sundry obiects they do ayme,
Yet all their studdies are bent to aspire
Unto *beatitude*? B. That you, said I,
Have this confirmed I remember well.
45   P. Dost not thou call to mind *beatitude*
To be a certaine *good*, and thereuppon
Wheras all men desire *felicity*,
All men to *goodnes* to attaine contend?
B. This thinge said I what neede I call to mynd?
50   Sith this, in memory, I fixed hould. /
P. All men therefore, both[10] *good, and bad* do strive
W^th one accord to gaine what thinge is good.
B. This consequent ariseth *naturall*,
Ph. But sure by gettinge *good, men are good made.*
55   B. Yes certainely. P. Good men therefore obtaine
What they do wish to have. B. So doth it seeme. /
P. But wicked men if they could app[re]hend
True goodnes wch they likewise covet, then
They could not evill be. B. It is right so.
60   P. Then wheras both of them, what *good* is, wish
But only one obtaine, the other not.
Can any doubt, y^t *good men puissant* be,
And *evil men* are curbed by *debility*?
B. Who doubteth this, said I, can neith[er] iudge
65   Of *natures* course, nor reasons consequence. /
P. Againe, *she* said, if two[11] men do propound

[9] desired] "o" *deleted after* "i" *MS*
[10] both] "o" *deleted after* "o" *MS*
[11] two] tow *MS*

One and the same exploit to undertake:
Of whom the one by *natures* benefit
The same beginninge, doth accomplish full,
70   The other destitute of *natures* helpe,
Is not of might the same to execute,
But doth by other meanes unnaturall
The doer imitate, yet not him match.
Wheth[er] of these more mightie may you iudge?
75   B. Allthough what you intend hence to informe
I do coniecture, yet heare more I would.
P. ffor men to walk, a moc[i]on naturall
To be, will you deny. B. No, in no wise.
P. Yf one then havinge use of feete should walke
80   Anoth[er] havinge not the benefite
Of feete by *nature*, should upon his hands
Endeavo[ur] for to walke, whether of these
More able to performe it can wee iudge?
B:[12] Assume the rest, said I, for no man doubts
85   The *Agent naturall*, to be of *might*
Much more then *he* who wanteth *natures aide*.
P:[13] But *soveraigne good*, w^ch *evil and good men*
Do both propound, only *good men* the same
By *vertues naturall* instinct, require:
90   But *evill men* by sundry appetits
Of greedy lusts, wch true *good* to obtain
Is nothinge *naturall*, do go about
The same to gaine. Do you thinke otherwise?
B. Not I for thence the consequent
95   Is evident, from former principles
W^ch I have granted, namely y^t *good men*
Are *mighty men*, and y^t *bad men* are weake.
P. Rightlie, said *she*, to *mind* thou dost revoke
W^ch is (accordinge to *Phisitians rule*)
100   A signe of *natures* forces rectified.
But now because to understand most prompt
I thee behould, I will not amplifie,
But breiflie will my reasons comp[re]hend.

---

[12] B.] *inserted in left margin*
[13] P.] *inserted in left margin*

Behould *bad mens infirmitie* appeares
105   In y^t, wherto intention *naturall*
          As by the hand doth leade, and urge by force,
          Therto they no way able are to reache.
          What may wee thinke of theire *debility*
          Yf wicked *men*, of *natures* benefit,
110   W^{ch} was ingrafted firme, deprived be.
          Consider furth[er] in the wicked traine
          What *imbillicity* doth still remaine. /
          For no small thinge it is that they would have,   36 ·[r]
          W^{ch} they cannot effect and bringe to passe:
115   But they do faile about the *supreme good*
          Of things, and cannot to the wished end
          Attaine, wherto they *night* and *day* contend,
          Wherin the strength of *good men*[14] doth excell.
          ffor as the man who walking on his feete,
120   Unto the place can reach, then wch no way
          Is further to be found, is thought to be
          Most able for to walke: Even so y^t man
          Who can to uttermost limyt of *good*,
          Beyond the wch no further *good can be*,
125   Aspire, most *mighty* him wee needs must iudge.
          ffrom whence the contrary wee may collect,
          Y^t *wicked men* are voyde of any *might*,
          For wherfore do they *vices* prosecute,
          Forsakinge *vertue*? Is it *ignorance*
130   Of what is *good*? But what more *impotent*
          Can be, then blindnes of base *ignorance*?
          Or what is to be followed do they know,
          And lust doth headlonge force them from the truth?
          So likewise by *intemperance* they *should*
135   Be of no *might*, who cannot conquere[15] *vice*. /
          Or do they willinglie, and wittinglie,
          The *good* forsake, and give themselves to *ill*:
          But so, not only[16] to be men of *might*
          They cease to be, but to be anythinge.

---

[14] men] *inserted above with caret*
[15] conquere] "e" *inserted above with caret after* "u"
[16] only] only *deleted after* only *MS*

140 ffor they who leave the common *end*[17] of all
  Y^t hath *a beinge*, cease to be at all. /
  W^{ch} thinge to some perhaps may seeme full strange,
  That *evill* men, who are the greater sort,
  To have no beinge, we should thus affirme. /
145 But so it is, for they y^t *evil* are,
  Them to be *evil* I do not deny:
  But I deny y^t merely and in truth
  They have any *existens*. ffor like as
  A carcas dead, a dead man you may call:
150 Simplie a man yet you may not him call.
  So wicked men I graunt they[18] *evill* are,
  But absolutely, y^t they beinge have,
  I may not grant. For y^t *existence* hath
  W^{ch} *order doth* retaine, *and nature keepes*,
155 But what therefrom doth swarve, relinquisheth
  That beinge, wch in *nature* proper was.
  But you will say, bad *men* can something do.   [36 v]
  I grant, but what they can effect
  Proceedeth not from *might* but *imbecillity*.
160 For *evill* they can bringe to pass at ease,
  Which they had not been able to effect,
  Yf y^t in doing *good* they could abide.
  I gath[er] then y^t they by such abilitie
  To do bad things, can nothing do at all. /
165 ffor if as wee before concluded have
  Evill is nothinge, then wheras they are
  Only of *might* to execute bad things:
  Y^t wicked men can nothing do it seemes. /
  B. It is most evident. *P*. But to the end
170 What might they have, you may now understand
  Wee have this thinge before determined,
  Y^t nothinge is more stronge then *supreme good*. /
  B: Tis true. *P*. But y^t cannot do evill. *B*. No.
  P. Doth any man suppose, y^t seely° men
175 Can all things do?[19] *B*. No man, except he dote.

---

[17] *end*] good *deleted with* end *inserted above with caret*
[18] they] ie *altered to* "y" *MS*
[19] do?] do. *MS*

P. But they can *evill do. B.* I would to *God*
They could not. Then wheras he can do all
Who can do what is *good*, but nothing so
It fareth[20] w^th *bad men*, who only *ill*
180   Are able to perform, it's manifest
Y^t such *bad men*, are weaker then the best:
Moreover, wee declared have before,
Y^t *mighty strength*, is to be numbered
Amongst such things as are to be required,
185   And that such things as wished are, to be,
To good, as unto *natures* certaine head,
Referred ought to be. But the *ability*
Of hainous crimes cannot be unto *good*
Referred then it is not to be wished
190   But *mighty* things are to be wished all.
Then whatsoever *wicked men* can do
May not be said to be a worke of *might*.
ffrom all wch proufs I gather the *ability*
Of *good men*, and *bad mens* most fraile *debilitie.*
195   The sentence is most true y^t *Plato* hath
That only wise men can effect such thinges
As they desire, but as for wicked men,
They exercise what thinges do serve their lust
But cannot satisfie theire myndes desire.
200   They do their appetit strive to fulfill,[21]
While as they thinke y^t *good* they can obtaine:
W^ch they desire by menes of theire *delights*,
     But they cannot attaine their wished end,
     For vice to happines cannot ascend.   37 ·[r]

Meter 2 ·
If any man might maskinge robes uncover
Of stately Kinges, who highe in regall seate
You do behould soaringe aloft to hover,
In glitteringe suites of purple shininge neate,
5   *Environed with armed souldiers sad,*
         Who are, with threatning lookes, and bloudshed mad

---

[20] fareth] "e" *deleted after* "f" *MS*
[21] fulfill] fuffill *MS*

He then may see
Such rulers to sustaine
Vice inwardly,
10   *Like bondes, them to detaine.*

For somtymes lusts torments their poysned hart,
Somtyme ire turbulent doth tosse their mind,
Somtime greife captivatinge makes them smart,
Vaine hope somtime doth vexe²² with passions blind.
15   *Then for so much as one man doth sustaine*
     So many tyrannizinge passions vaine:
       He cannot do
     What he would faine effect,
       Oppress'd so
20   *Affections him deiect.*

Prose 3 · /

Wherefore, in what mire ignominious
Vices²³ are rowled do you not behould?
And in what excellencie *virtue* shines?
Wherefrom ariseth consequents most plaine,
5   Yᵗ *godly men do never* want rewards,
Nor *wicked men do* punishments escape.
ffor of the things wᶜʰ *men* attempt to do,
That thinge, for wᶜʰ another thinge is done,
It seemes therof to be a recompence. /
10   As unto him that in a *Race* doth run[n]e,
The *Game*, for wᶜʰ he run[n]es, his *guerdon*° is.
But yᵗ *beatitude* is such a *good*
For wᶜʰ *alone* all enterprises²⁴ are
Attempted, I before²⁵ declared have,
15   Then unto humaine Action *very good*
As *guerdon*° *common* unto all is sett,
But from *good men* this parted cannot be.
ffor why? Such man may not be called *good*,

---

²² *vexe*] *inserted above with caret*
²³ Vices] *letter deleted after* "i" *with* "c" *inserted above*
²⁴ enterprises] "r" *deleted after third* "e" *MS*
²⁵ before] there *deleted before* "f" *with* be *inserted above*

Who wantteth *goodnes*, wherefore iust rewards   [37 v]
20   Do not forsake mens *manners Vertuouse*. /
      Let *wicked men* then rage never so much,
      Yet wise mens *crowne* doth not decay nor fade,
      Nor wickednes, wch is from *goodnes* strange,
      Can from *good myndes* their proper *Guerdon*° steale.
25   But if *impietie* should vainely boast
      Of y^t wch it receives extrinsecall,
      Eyth[er] anoth[er], or he y^t[26] it gave,
      Againe may such externall thinges revoke.
      But sith reward men gaine by pietie,
30   Y^t fayleth then, when *men* faile *good* to be. /
      Lastlie wheras *every* reward is sought
      Because it is supposed to be *good*,
      What man will iudge him, who doth *good* enioy,
      To be w^thout reward? But what reward?
35   Most beautifull and greatest guift of all.
      For call to *mind* my *corallary* late.
      W^ch I thee gave as a cheife consequent,
      And argue thus: wheras *beatitude*
      Is verie *good*, y^t *good men* blessed all[27]
40   Become, in y^t they *good* are, it is plaine[28]
      Now they who *blessed* are, they *Gods* become,
      The crowne then of the *good* is to be *Gods*
      W^ch *crowne* no day can wast, nor *might* can spoile,
      Or *mans impietie* can put to foile. /
45   W^ch beinge so a wise man cannot doubt:
      Of bad mens punishment inseperable. /
      ffor wheras *good and evill* do dissent,
      And punishments and guifts contrary are,
      What thinge touchinge the *Guerdon*° of *good men*
50   Wee see to come to passe, the same must be
      Full correspondent on the adverse parte,
      By any meanes in bad mens punishment.
      Then as to *good men goodnes* is reward,

---

[26] y^t] *word deleted after* y^t *MS*
[27] all] become *deleted after* all *MS*
[28] it is plaine] they Gods become *deleted with* it is plaine *inserted above with caret*

So to²⁹ the *bad* theire *vice* is punishment.
55 Now who so is crossed wᵗʰ punishment
He doubteth not yᵗ *evill* doth him vexe.
Wherefore if they themselves examine would
No punishment to have can they account,
Whom vilest *vice* not only doth deiect
60 But doth excedinglie wᵗʰ sores infect?
But further see contrary to the *good*,
What punishment attendeth on the *bad*.   38 [r]
ffor all things having *beinge* you are taught
Are one, wᶜʰ one is *good*, from whence it is
65 Yᵗ every thinge yᵗ is, seemes to be *good*.
Then whatsoever fayleth to be *good*,
The same thinge ceaseth for to be at all.
ffrom whence it followeth yᵗ *wicked men*
Do cease to be, what thinge they were before.
70 But yᵗ they have ben men their humaine shape
Remaininge still doth manifestlie showe.
Wherefore they turninge into *wickednes*,
Their former *humaine nature* they do loose.
But for so much as *only honestie*
75 Can man above *mans dignitie* promote,
It necessarylie doth follow hence,
Impiety below mans worth detruds
Them, whom it doth from *humaine* state deiect.
Then *metamorphosed* whom you do see
80 By *vices*, iudge not him a man to be.
Doth violent *Extorters* of *mens goods*
Wᵗʰ gredy appetit inflamed rage?
Like raveninge *wolfe* you may such man esteeme.
Ys any feirce and turbulent, whose tounge
85 Wᵗʰ brawlinge controversies is defiled?
Him comparable to a *dogge* account.
Doth any secretlie reioyce to lurke
In privie corneʳˢ wᵗʰ fraude to purloine?
Such *man to foxes you may equalize.*
90 Doth any man intemperatelie chase?
The *lions mind* to beare he may be thought.

---

²⁹ to] *inserted above with caret*

Is any timorous[30] and fugitive
Trembling at y^t w^ch *he* ought not to feare?
Like to the *stagges* in cowardice he stands.

95   Is any slowe of dull and drowsie spirit?
A life he leades not differinge from the *Asse.* /
Light and inconstant doth his *mind* still change?
From flittinge foules he doth nothinge dissent. /
W^th foule and filthie lust is he bemyr'd?

100   W^th stinckinge swines delight he taynted is.
So com[m]eth it to passe y^t every *man*
Who, *honestie* forsakinge, doth surcease
To be a man, because he cannot reach
        To be transformed into *divine nature,*

105   He changed is into a beastlie *creature.*   [38 v]

                    Meter 3 · /

The wind, Ulisses tossed shipps, did drive
On surginge Seas unto a strange Iland,
After his wandering longe, who did arive
Where Goddes Circes regall seate did stand,

5   *From Sol descended, who with charmes doth strive*
Prepared cups to offer with her hand
        To guests arrivinge new as they resort,
        Changinge their shapes with skill in sundry sort. /

Deformed shape of Bore some do retaine,
10   *Like lion feirce wth teeth and pawes some growe,*
Like howlinge wolfe complaninge some remaine,
To howse some tame like Indian Tygers go.
Though Mercury unloose him from her chaine
And in his many troubles pittie show,

15   *The rest yet of Ulisses men from harme*
            Not so secured tasted of her charme.

Who unto Swine transform'd on acornes fed,
W^ch they were faine instead of breade to chew:
Whose wonted voice, and body vanished,
20   *Their mynd alone unchanged grones to veiwe*

---

[30] timorous] "o" *inserted above with caret after* "m"

Their owne deformed shape so altered. /
O feble charmes! Small change could thence ensue,
   Though members they can chaunge from nature kind,
   Yet are unable to transforme mans mynd. /

25   *Vigor of man is seated in the hart*
       Internally conveyed farre from sight,
       Placed in Turret stronge by Natures art
       Free from such incantations dreadfull might,
       The secret poyson of vile vices dart,
30   *Rather transformeth man with subtill slight.*
         And though mans body be conserved sound
         Yet savage vices charmes mans minde doth wounde. /

Prose 4 ·

These yo[ur] assertions I grant, said I,
Nor wthout cause I see y^t *vicious men*
Allthough still humaine *shape* they do retaine,
Are said to be transformed into beasts,
5   By reason of their qualitie of *mynd.*
But y^t the savage and ungodlie *mynd,*
Unto the hurt of *good men* should so rage,
I would they had not so much libertie.   39 [r]
P. Noe liberty, said *she,* theirin they have,
10   As shall be proved in convenient place,
But if y^t thinge wch is imagined
Lawfull for them to be, removed were,
A great parte of the punishment most iust
Of wicked men theirby should be releived.
15   For y^t wch seemes incredible to some,
Ungodlie men are more unfortunate,
When they their lust and wishes execute,
Then if those hainous Acts wch they desire
They were not able for to bringe to passe.
20   For if to have a will to wicked things
Be misery, then to be of might
To execute the same, more wretched is
Wthout the wch th'effect of wretched will
Is of noe force. Then for as much
25   As in these severally is misery

W^th threfould wretchednes they vexed are
Whom you behould, *to will to be of might*,
And to effect the thinge, y^t wicked is.
B. I yeild hereto, said I, but I do wish

30   From hart, they should quicklie deprived be
Of such misfortune, and y^t they should want
Abilitie to compasse wicked acts.
P.^31 They shall therof soner deprived be
Then you perhaps will eyth[er] wish, or they

35   Them selves suppose they shall be destitute.
For nothinge is in lymits short of life
So durable, y^t mans im[m]ortall mynd
Should make account hereto continue longe. /
Of wch bad men the expectac[i]on greate

40   And highe attempts of their *godlesse exploits*,
W^th suddaine and unlooked for event,
It oftentymes made frustrate of their hopes. /
W^ch is to them an end of misery.
For if *ungodlines* men wretched make,

45   The more they are in miserable case
By how much more their vice continueth. /
Whom most unfortunate I should esteeme
Yf y^t their wickednes by death at last
(Yf not before) should not be finished.

50   For if of the misfortune of vile vice,
Wee have the truth by demonstrac[i]on shewed
It needs must be an endles misery,
W^ch is protracted to eternitie. /
B. A strange and difficult conclusion

55   This is to be by man subscribed too.   [39 v]
But to the p[re]misses granted before
This consequent doth well agre, I know.
P. You iudge aright, but who so doth esteeme
It difficult to grant a *consequent*,

60   It is required y^t he demonstrate
Eyth[er] the *antecedent* to be false,
Or els the *propositions disposition.*
To be inartificially fram'd

---

^31 *P.*] *inserted in left margin*

So as from thence a necessary drift
65   Of sound conclusion cannot be deduced,
For otherwise yf y^t the *premisses*
Be granted to be true, ther is no cause
Why one should doubt of the *conclusions* clause. /
But this also wch I will now declare
70   No lesse to be admyred may appeare
But from y^t wch before assumed is
It is as necessary. *B.* What is that?
P. That men unhonest are more happie farre
When they sustaine deserved punishment
75   Then if no penaltie inflicted were. /
But I intend not now y^t to conclude
W^{ch} every man doth plainelie beare in mynd,
Y^t manners of bad men corrected are
By punishments, and by the feare therof
80   Are terrified and unto *good* reclaim'd
And unto oth[ers] are examples made,
For to avoyde what thinge is worthie blame.
But I account y^t by anothers means
Unhonest men much more unhappie are
85   When as they do unpunished escape,
Though their correction, and examples theirs,
Wee cease to urge, nor have therof respect.
B. What oth[er] meanes of proufe besides these is?
P. That *good men* happie are, and *evill men*
90   Are wretched have not we concluded? *B.* Yes.
P. Yf then, said *she*, unto mans misery
Some *good* annexed be, is not his state
More happie, then the miserie of such
W^{ch} merely wretched are, voyd of all good
95   Mixture wherof may miseries asswage.
B. It seemeth so. *P.* What if y^t wretched man
Who destitute of all good things remaines
Another *evill* have annexed more,
Is not he to be thought a wretched man
100   Much more unhappie then the other is,
Whose misery by mixture of some *good*
Asswaged is? *B.* Good reason so, said I.   40 [r]
P. Now wicked men sustaininge punishment

Some *good* to them therby annexed have,
105   Namely the punishment it selfe, wch is
Yf you respect the iustice, a *good thinge.* /
And when such men unpunished escape
Therby to them some evill added is,
To wit *impunity,* wch you confesse
110   And not unworthelie, y^t it is *ill.*
B. I cannot it deny. *P.* Then wicked men
Escapinge by uniust *impunity,*
Are more unhappie, then when punished
By iust severity they are restrain'd.
115   But it is evident y^t wicked *men*
To be chasticed is a righteous Act,
And them to be unpunished is wronge.
B. Who can deny it? *P.* But anoth[er] thinge
No man can well deny, y^t what is iust
120   The same must needs be *good* in any case,
Contrariwise what is uniust, is *ill.*
B. ffrom former sentences concluded, these
By necessary consequents arise. /
But I besech you, do you make account
125   After the body is by death surprised
The souls of men no punishment sustaine?
P. Yea, punishment they suffer very great. /
Wherof I thinke some exercised are
W^th endless torments sharpe austeritie:
130   Others are purged not wth such severity. /
But in this place, concerninge punishments
Of this kinde to dispute, I purpose not. /
I hitherto have only enterprized
Y^t you may understand y^t all the power
135   Of wicked men wch did appeare to you
To be unworthie most, is non at all. /
And y^t whom you complained to escape
Unpunished, you might behould, y^t they
Reape punishment for their *ungodlines.*
140   And y^t the libertie wch you did pray
Might quicklie come to end, you might perceive
Not to be longe, and if it should be longe,
So much the more unhappie it should be. /

And most unhappie if it had no end.

145 ffurther y^t wicked men more wretched are
When they uniustlie range unpunished,
Then when by iust revenge they are supprest. /
Wherto this consequent inferred stands,
Y^t then they greater punishment sustaine,   [40 v]
150 When they are thought to be unpunished. /
B. When as your former reasons I behould
Nothinge more true then theise things are, I iudge:
But when to humaine iudgement I returne,
What man is he, not only who beleves
155 These proposic[i]ons, but who will them heare? /
P. It is right so, for they cannot errect
Theire eies, to darknes blind accustomed,
To veiwe the light of truth perspicuous.°
But are like *owles*, whose eyes[32] the night
160 Illuminateth, but the day doth blind.
ffor while they *looke* not on the course of things,
But only their affections do behould,
They iudge y^t licence and *impunity*
Offences to commit is happie state. /
165 But what the law eternall ratifieth
Observe, if unto *vertues excellent*
The *minde* thou shalt addict, thou shalt not neede
To have a *iudge* to offer thee reward,
Thou shalt thy selfe make equall to the *Gods*.
170 Yf unto *vices* vile thou give thy *mynd*,
Externall punisher thou needs not seeke,
Thy selfe like to the beasts thou dost debase. /
Like as if you by courses mutuall
The abiect earth, and heavens highe behould
175 Allthough externall iudgements do surcease,
Yet you by reason sole of sight shall seeme
Somtyme the clay sometyme the starres to touch.
But vulgar sort these things do not respect.
What then? Shall wee to them yeild o[ur] consent,
180 Whom wee to be as beasts declared have?[33]

---

[32] eyes] *erasure over-written*
[33] have?] have. *MS*

What if a man deprived whole of sight
Y^t he hath had his sight, should quite forget
And should suppose y^t he doth nothinge want
To humaine complements perfection?
185   May wee not thinke y^t they who iudge the same
Are also blind themselves? For com[m]on sort
Of *men* herto will by no meanes subscribe,
W^{ch} builded standes uppon like stable ground
Of reason strong, that they who offer wrong
190   Are more unhappie by many degres,
Then such men are who suffer iniuries. /
B: These reasons yo[urs] to heare I much expect.
P. Can you deny y^t every wicked man
Deserveth punishment to have[?][34] *B*. Fy no.
195   *P*. But it is many waies made evident
Y^t they who wicked are, unhappie are.   41 [r]
B. Most true it is. *P*. Then they who punishment
Deserve, you doubt not but they wretched are.
B. These things wth truth accord. *P*. Yf then you were
200   An *Arbitrator* sett in *iudgment* seate,
Whom will you iudge ought to be punished
Him y^t did offer, or y^t suffered wronge.
B. I would not study longe to satisfie
The man who had sustayned iniury,
205   By punishinge the *doer* of the wronge.
P. Then he more wretched far to you should seeme
Who doth infer, then *he* who suffered wronge. /
B. The consequent is *good. P*. Wherefore by this
And such like reasons builded on this ground
210   Y^t foule dishonestie, by *nature* doth
Make men to be in miserable cause.
It doth appeare y^t offred iniury
To any man is not so much a wronge
To the receiver, as to the offerer. /
215   But now o[ur] *Orators* deale otherwise
For they for such as suffer violence,
The *Iudges* to excite to pittie strive
When as the trespasser much rath[er] ought

---

[34] have[?]] have *MS*

By iust compassion to be pytied
220   Who rath[er] ought to *iudgment* to be brought
As *patients* sicke to the *Phisitian*,
By such accusers as would pittie them,
And not in heate of choller them accuse.
Y^t they by punishment might extirpate
225   And launce the wound of their com[m]itted cryme.
W^{ch} thing observed, the defenders ayde
Would either wholely languishe wthout use,
Or if to do them *good* they rather wish,
Then their defense of such they should convert
230   Into the *habit* of accusing them. /
Allso such *wicked men* yf they could frame
Their sight of *mind* in some measure to veiwe,
Beauty of *vertue*, whom they did forsake
And would consider y^t by punishments
235   They shall the staines of *vices* wash away,
And may thereby to honestie aspire,   [41 v]
Their chasticements they would not tortures count,
Defenders paines they also would refuse,
And to Accusers, and to Iudges will
240   They wholely would them selves therin com[m]it. /
Wherby it comes to passe y^t wth wise men
No place at all for hatred can be left. /
ffor who, except he be a blockish foole,
Will hate *good men*? And *evil men* to hate
245   Were as absurd and void of reasons ground.
ffor as mans body hath infirmities
So vice is as the sicknes of the *mynd*.
Now sith sicke *men* in body non doth hate,
But rath[er] such wth pittie we behould:
250   Much more such *wicked men*, whose sickly mynds
Impiety more feirce then any paines,
        Molesteth mightely, we should not hate:
        But rather them wth teares commiserate. /

Meter 4 ·
What gaineth man deadly tumults to breede?
And fate to instigate with his owne hand?
If death you seeke, death doth approach wth speede,

Whose horses swiftlie coursinge never stand.
5   *Whom Serpent, Lion, Tiger, Beare, and Bore,*
          With tooth assaile, with sword men punish more.

Do men attempt uniust and savage warre,
And wish to slay each other mutually,
Because their soile and manners differ farre?
10   *Thes are no reasons sound of cruelty.*
          Would you to all men iust deservinges give,
          Love godly men, and for the[35] *godles live.*

Prose 5 ·
ffrom hence what happines, or misery
Consisteth in the merits of the *good*,
As also of the *bad*, I do behould. /
Yet in mans common ſortune I p[er]ceive
5   Some *good* or *evill* therein to inhere.
ffor noe wise man will rather chouse to be
Banished, poore, and ignominious,   42 ·[r]
Then to excell in wealth and dignitie,
To be of powerfull strength, and to remayne
10   In his own native Citty florishinge.
ffor so more clearely and apparently
His wisdomes office he may execute.
ffor in some sort *Rulers beatitude*
Transferred is to forreine *Nations*.
15   Wheras especially imprisonment,
The law, and legall penalties, are due
Rath[er] to Citizens pernicious.
For whose default they constituted were. /
Wherefore I much admyre why these events
20   Unequally wth course reciprocall
Are chaunged so, y^t *vices* punishments
Oppresse *good men*, and wicked men do reape
Vertues reward. And I request of you
To understand what may the reason be
25   Of such uniust and strange confusion.
ffor lesse should I admire, if I did iudge

---

[35] *the*] *they* MS

All things by *fortunes* changes mixed were:
But *God* now beinge governo[ur] of all
This my astonishment doth aggravate.
30   Who for as much as oft he doth impart
To *good men* pleasures, and to *bad men* smart.
Contrariwise to *godly men* sometymes
He sendeth crossing tribulac[i]ons,
And to men wicked their desires doth graunt.
35   Unles the cause hereof wee can p[er]ceive,
What may be thought herein to disagree
From *fortunes* fickle mutability?
P. No marvile if some things confused seeme,
While men are ignorant of y^t highe cause
40   Whereby *God* doth in order all dispose.
     Yet[36] sith the world is guided by *Gods might*,
     Doubt not but all things do succeede aright. /

Meter 5 ·

Arcturus starres if any do not know
Neare to the Articke pole fixed to move,
Skies rules admyreth, why Bootes slow
In our Horizon tarieth longe above
5   *Drivinge his wayne,° not hidden longe in Sea,*
     He streightway doth him selfe in sight display.   [42 v]

The hornes of full Moone darkned pale do growe,
Ecclipsed in the tyme of gloumy night:
Whose dimmed light discovered starres doth show,
10   *Whom Phœbe shininge bright had hid from sight.*
     From hence Error doth many Nations move,
     With bels and basons Moones charmes to remove.

But non admireth that the blusteringe blasts
Doth beate the shore with fominge waves and stormes,
15   *Nor that congeled snow drift quickly wasts,*
     Dissolved by bright scorchinge Phœbus beames. /

---

[36] Yet] *word deleted after* Yet MS (Yet *was inscribed in the indentation just to the left of the deleted word*)

> *For, in thes last examples cyted here,*
> *Do certaine causes evident appeare.*

> *The other former causes hidden are,*
20 *Which to find out most mindes of men torment:*
> *Knowledge wherof lately found out is rare,*
> *And common sort admire such strange event. /*
> *If mistie ignorance depart from mynd,*
> *Nothinge to be admired shall we finde. /*

Prose 6 ·

These things are true, said I, but for as much
As causes of things secret to discusse,
And reasons hid in darknes to revayle,
Unto yo[ur] selfe by right doth appertaine:
5   I now besech you these things to decide,
And me herin instruct. For this strang thinge
Above all other doth amazement bringe.
She somewhat smyling then, thus answered.
P. To matter most profound and intricate
10   You me insight, wch to determine full
And finde the deepth therof what can suffice. /
For such a thinge[37] it is, y^t as one doubt
Resolved is, innumerable mo,
Like heads of *Hydra*, do againe arise.
15   Neither will any limyts this containe,
Unles wth prudence one the same restraine. /
ffor in this cause wee are accustomed
Of the *symplicity* of providence
For to propound great disputac[i]on,   43 ·[r]
20   Also concerninge fatall causes course,
Concerninge chaunces casuall events,
Of *Gods* foreknowledge, and p[re]destinac[i]on,
Concerninge freedom of the will of man.
Which thinge of what importance and what weight
25   They are, you do observe. But for so much
As no small porc[i]on of yo[ur] medicyn
This is for you to understand these things,

---

[37] a thinge] a thinge *deleted after* a thinge MS

Allthough[38] environed wth narrow bounds
Of tyme wee are, yet will wee undertake
30   Something hereof now to deliberate.
But if you do in verses musicall
Take *delectac[i]on*, yet such pleasures yo[urs]
You must a while forebeare untill such tyme
As I shall have propounded Arguments
35   In order lincked wth fitt consequents. /
B. Do what you please, said I, then *she* began
As if new matter *she* would undertake. /
And thus *she* did dispute. *P.* The generac[i]on
Of every thing, as also every chaunge
40   Of things y^t are by *nature* mutable,
And what so moved is in any wise,
Receiveth causes, order, and their formes,
From the stability of *mynd divine.* /
W^{ch} beinge seated in the turret highe
45   *Of Gods simplicity* determineth
Meanes manifould of executing things. /
W^{ch} meanes when as it is considered
Accordinge as it is, in divine purity
Of *Gods* intelligence, it named is
50   *His providence.* / But when relac[i]on
It hath to those affaires wch it doth move
And doth dispose in orders regiment,
Then fate it called is of th'Auncient. /
W^{ch} to be things distinct may plaine appeare,
55   Yf y^t the efficacy[39] of them both
A man consider by the sight of *mynd.*
For providence is y^t reason divine
W^{ch} constituted is in *supreme Prince,*   [43 v]
Of all wch doth all things disposinge guide. /
60   But fate is such a disposic[i]on
W^{ch} doth in transitory things consist,
Whereby *Gods providence* uniteth all
In order severall firme to where [each is].[40] /

---

[38] Allthough] *letter deleted after final "h" MS*
[39] efficacy] *ic inserted above with caret*
[40] each is] *emendation to complete sentence [Latin: ... fatum vero inhaerens rebus mobilibus dispositio per quam providentia suis quaeque nectit ordinibus.]*

ffor *providence* doth all things comp[re]hend,
65   As if they were all one, allthough they be
Distinguished, though infinit they were.
But *fate* things severall distributinge
Into their moc[i]ons, places, formes, and tymes,
Them doth digest, wch explicac[i]on
70   Of order temporall considered
As in *Gods* knowledge it doth stand foreseene,
It is his providence: but the same union
As it divided is and in due tymes
Reveyled, so it may be called fate. /
75   W^{ch} though they be distinct, yet doth the one
Of these uppon the other still depend.
ffor fatall order ever springeth hence,
From the simplicity of providence.
ffor like as the *Artificer*, the forme
80   Of what he would have finished in mynd
Retainyng, doth the workes effect attempt.
And what he simplie, and in one instant
Of tyme foresawe, he doth in tyme produce.
Likewise doth *God* by divine providence
85   By one sole Act most steadfastlie dispose
Of what is to be put in execuc[i]on. /
But those things wch he so disposed hath,
By many meanes and seasons severall,
By course of *fate* he doth administer.
90   Then whether *fate* by certaine *divine spirits*
Attendant on *Gods providence* doth stand,
Wheth[er] the soule, or *Natures* entire frame,
Serve therunto, or influence of starres,
Celestiall in firmament who move
95   Whether the course of *fate* united is
By *Angels* regiment, or spirits skill:
Wheth[er] by some of these, or ells by all.
Yet this is manifest y^t *providence*
Is the im[m]oveable and simple forme
100   Of all things wch are to be brought to passe. /
But *fate* of those things wch simplicity
Of divine providence determined
To be effected, is the mutable

44 ·[r]

Connecting of the same in tract of tyme. /
105   Wherby it is y^t what things unto fate
        Are subiect, they likewise to providence
        Subiected stand, to whom *fate* also yeildes.
        But certaine things wch under providence
        Contained are, surpasse the course of fate.
110   Such are those things wch fixed stedfastly
        Adioyninge neare to *nature* most *divine*
        Order of fatall levity surmount. /
        ffor like as of these *orbes* wch rowled are
        About the *Pole*, y^t wch is innermost
115   Is nearest to the meanes stability,
        And as it were a center to the rest,
        W^ch from the same are placed further of,
        The furthermost wherof turned about
        W^th greater circuit, by how much it is
120   Distant from the *Poles* point indivisible,
        By so much more it doth in ample course
        Of larger space extend his moc[i]ons.
        But if unto the middle point of *Pole*
        Shall any thinge it selfe associate,
125   Therto united fast, it doth become
        Immutable,[41] and ceaseth to extend
        His wandring courses moving far and wide,
        In like sort what thinge further doth depart
        From *Gods* stabilitie of *mind most sovereigne*,
130   In greater *laborinth* of ficle *fate*
        Insnared is, and so much more from *fate*
        A thinge exempted is, by how much more
        Neare to the center of *Gods* maiestie
        He doth approach, but if it shall cleve fast
135   To the stabilitie of *supreme minde*,
        So shall it not by wanderinge moc[i]ons raunge
        But shall surmount the toyle of fatall chaung.   [44 v]
        The movinge order of *fates* mutability
        Compared to the pure stabilitie
140   Of *providence divine*, hath like proporc[i]on
        As *myndes* discourse hath to the intellect,

---

[41] Immutable] ImMutable *MS*, Im *inserted in left margin*

Or that wch framed is by *generation*
To y^t wch hath his *beinge* permanent,
Or tymes succession to *eternity*,
145   Or as a circle to the middle point. /
This course of *fatall destiny* doth move
Heaven and *constellations* of the starres,
And *Elements* doth temper mutuall
By commutac[i]on reciprocall,
150   Who doth transforme their qualities and formes. /
The same concourse of *fate* doth still renue
All things y^t do begine, or cease to live,
By like progresse of *issue* and of seede.
Mans Actions all and *fortunes fate* doth bynd
155   By indissoluble causes connection,
Whych⁴² for so much as they proceding have
From principles of stable providence,
W^{ch} in it selfe unchangeable doth stande,
They needs must be them selves unchangable.
160   ffor so should things be best administred
Yf singlenes abyding in *Gods* mynd
Immutable orders of causes all
Produce, wch order should such things restraine,
W^{ch} els would rashly changinge still remaine.
165   Whereby it comes to passe, y^t though we can
By no meanes understand this course of things
So as all seeme confused out of frame,
Yet not wthstandinge course of providence
Disposeth all, directinge it to *good*.
170   ffor nothing is for *evills* sake performed.
No not so much as of unhonest men,
Whom as abundantlie we have declared
Ayminge at *good*, vile *Error* doth seduce. /
Much lesse fatall decree wch doth proceede
175   From center of cheife *goodnesse* can wthdraw
Any from his *begininges supreme lawe*. /
But you will say what strange confusion
Can more iniuriouslie be suffered,
Then y^t to *good men* both *adversity*,   45 [r]

---

⁴² Whych] ch *inserted above with caret*

180   And prosperous events should so succede:
        And y^t to *evill men prosperitie*,
        And odious afflictions should fall.
        Are men of such integritie of *mynd*
        Y^t whom they shall iudge to be *good* or *bad*
185   They needes must be such as they be esteem'd?
        But herein mans opinion dive^{rs} is
        And whom some do account worthie rewards,
        Others esteeme them worthie punishment,
        But let us here admit y^t any man
190   Were able to discerne *good men* from *bad*
        Can he behould internall temperature
        Of *mindes* (as men of bodies use to speake)
        For myracle not much unlike to this
        It is to them who did not know the cause,
195   Whie unto healthie bodies should agree
        To some men sweete, to oth[ers] bitter things,
        Why sicke men also some wth sweete receipts,
        And some wth sowre restored are to health.
        But the *Phisitian* who doth conceive
200   Of health and sicknes cause and qualities
        These things doth not in any case[43] admire.
        What other thinge doth soules health seeme to be
        Then honestie? What oth[er] thinge then vice
        Is the disease therof? Now who beside
205   Y^t *God*, who governeth and healeth *mindes*,
        P[re]serveth *good* men,[44] and restraineth *bad*?
        Who when as from highe glasse of *providence*
        He lokinge downe, doth clearely understande
        W^{ch} is convenient for everyone:
210   To all he doth applie what seemeth fitt. /
        ffrom hence y^t Miracle of *fatall* course
        Doth growe, when that by *Gods knowledge* is wrought,
        W^{ch} to men ignorant amazement brought.
        Now y^t I breiflie may conclude, so far
215   As humaine reason able is to search,
        Touchinge the deepth of *divine* secrecies:

---

[43] case] "u" *deleted after* "a" *MS*
[44] men] *inserted above with caret*

That man whom you most iust and righteous
Esteeme, to *Gods* allseinge providence
Accounted is to be farr otherwise.
220   As *Lucan* o[ur] familier contreman
Admonished y^t *Cæsars conqueringe* cause   [45 v]
Pleased the *Gods*, but *Cato* did approve
The cause of *Pompey* beinge conquered. /
Then whatsoever in the world you see
225   Besides mans expectac[i]on to be done,
Order in such things doth proceede aright,
Allthough it seeme disorder in thy sight. /
But graunt y^t some man is so vertuous
Y^t in the iudgment[45] both of *God* and *Men*
230   He is pronounced to be righteous
Yet in his strength of *mynd* he is infirme,
So as in him adversitie should vey,
Perhaps his innocency he might forsake,
Esteeming y^t the cause of his mishap.
235   Such man the prudent dispensac[i]ons
Of *God* doth spare, whom such adversitie
Crossinge would make much worse, lest unto whom
Afflicc[i]ons are unfit, he might oppresse. /
Another man wth *vertues* absolute
240   In life sincere, and neare to *God*, there is
Him to be touched wth afflicc[i]ons
Of any kinde, *Gods* providence doth iudge
A thing unlawfull, so as not so much
As wth diseases bodily to be
245   Afflicted he will suffer such a man. /
ffor as a certaine man most excellent
Hath witnessed y^t *vertues* edifie
The body of a man religious
Moreover oftentymes it comes to passe
250   Y^t to *good men supreme authority*
Of government for great cause is convey'd
Y^t *vice* aboundinge may therby be staye'd. /
To some he distributs now *good* now bad,
According to the quality of *mindes*,

---

[45] iudgment] "g" *inserted above with caret*

255   Some he wth woes doth pinch lest they grow proud
       By longe prosperity. Some he permits
       Wth hard mishaps tossed to be turmoyl'd
       Y^t they therby the *vertues* of their *mind*
       By exercise of patience might confirme. /
260   Some overmuch do feare to undertake
       What thinge they well are able to effect.
       Others p[re]suming make too small account
       Of that wch they unable are to beare.   46 ·[r]
       These for the triall of their ablenes
265   *God* leadeth into many crosses sharpe.
       Some men have purchased wth costlie price
       Of glorious death a reverend name on earth.
       Some men unconquered⁴⁶ by punishments
       Have shew'd example unto other men,
270   Y^t *vertue* doth invincyble remayne,
       Never subdued by the wicked trayne. /
       Of all wch things their is no question
       Y^t rightlie and in orders harmony
       And for the benefite of them, to whom
275   These seeme to chaunce, they executed are. /
       By wch said resons it may proved be
       Y^t to the wicked sometymes miseries,
       And sometyme wished things to them succeede.
       Concerning miseries no man admyres
280   For all iudge them to have deserved ill:
       Whose punishments not only terryfie
       Others from hanyous crymes pernicious,
       But also mend them who are punished.
       But the prosperitie of wicked men
285   Great Argument to *good men* doth afford
       What they should thinke of such felicity,
       W^{ch} they behould to wayte on *evill men.*
       Wherin I iudge *God* wiselie doth dispose
       Y^t wheras some⁴⁷ are of such nature rash
290   And so intemperatly importunate,
       Y^t povertie would make them sharper sett

---

⁴⁶ unconquered] un *inserted above with caret*
⁴⁷ some] men *deleted after* some MS

Headlonge to rushe into most vile attempts:
This sicknes *providence* doth wisely cure
By remedie of giving such man wealth.
295   Such wicked man seinge his conscience
Wth crymes polluted and shall wth him selfe
Compare theirwth his *fortune* prosperous,
Perhaps will feare lest sorrowfull he loose
The thinge wher of he hath the ioyfull use.
300   ffor wch cause⁴⁸ he will chaunge his manners bad
And while his former fortune he shall feare
To loose, his wickednes he⁴⁹ will forbeare. /
Some beinge rays'd unworthelie to top
Of great prosperitie, are headlong cast
305   Into deserved infelicitie. /   [46 v]
To some authoritie of punishinge
Permitted is, y^t it might be the meanes
To exercise the vertues of the *good*:
And wth greate punishments to curb the *bad*. /
310   ffor as no leauge concordant there can be
Betwen the honest and unhonest mynds,
So neither can unhonest men agree
Betwen themselves. And greatest reason why
For whereas vyces do distract the mynde,
315   One from another, they do still dissent.
And oftentymes such things they enterprice
W^{ch} when to end they have accomplished,
They iudge it fit to be relinquished.
ffrom whence the *highest providence*, oft tymes
320   A myracle prodigious doth produce,
Y^t wicked men, do make the wicked, *good*.
ffor when men seeme to beare indignities
By bad men offred, then inflam'd wth hate
Of such unhonest men, who them afflict,
325   To vertue profitable they returne,
Because they study from them to dissent
Whom they do hate. ffor only divine power
Ys such y^t it can *evill* turne to *good*.

---

⁴⁸ cause] *inserted above with caret*
⁴⁹ he] *letter deleted after* "e" *MS*

When as in fittest seasons usinge them
330   Th'effect of some *good*, it doth picke therefrom.
ffor certaine order comp[re]hendeth all
Y^t what thinge shall in any sort decline
From course assigned by *Gods providence*,
Allthoughe the same to other course revolt
335   Yet into order it constrayned is.
Lest in the kingdomes rule of providence
Should any priviledge be left for chaunce.
The strongest *God* throughout the world, all those
Divers events to *good end* doth dispose,
340   But unto man it is no lawfull thinge
By shallow witt either to comp[re]hend
Or els in baren words to explicate
Order and causes all of *worke divine*. /
This only to behould let it suffice,
345   Y^t *God* who hath produced *natures* all,
Directinge all to *good* doth them dispose,
And while the things wch he produced hath   47 ·[r]
He doth endeavo[ur] to retaine in good
Accordinge to his owne similitude,
350   All *evill* from the *lymits* of his *Realme*
By fatall order he will extirpate:
Whereby it is y^t *evills* all, wch seeme
In earth most to abound, if you respect
Disposinge providence you shall perceive
355   Nothing at all may anywhere seem *ill*.
But I you see allreadie weried
W^th questions weight, and Arguments prolixe,
Expect some ease by verses melodie.
        Whereof a tast receive, thy mynd to feede,
360   Whereby more stronge wee further may proceede.

                    Meter 6 · /
With prudent mind if you would clearely see
The reigiment of highest power divine,
Attentively then do your eies incline
To view the stately tops of heavens highe.
5   *For in firme leauge, wch doth not flittinge swerve,*
        The starres their auncient harmony observe.

The blazinge beames of Phœbus bright as fire
Do never hinder th'orbe of Phœbe cold,
Nor Urse Maior whose swifte course doth hould
10   Bendinge about Pole Articke, doth desire
          To dippe his flaminge light in Ocean deepe,
          Though other starres, hee see, that course do keepe. /

Bright eveninge Vessper orderly doth show
With equall space of tyme that night is neare:
15   And Lucifer doth bringe the morninge cleare,
So love by course alternally doth goe,
          Revivinge endles courses mutually,
          So discourd none doth harbour in the sky. /

This concord equalizeth elements
20   In even balances, that contraries
As moist to dry thinges yeild by fitt degrees,
And cold with heate combin'd it selfe contents:
          That mountinge fire ascendeth up on highe,
          And massie earth discendinge low doth ly. /   [47 v]

25   By this concordinge harmony, in Springe
The yeare sweete flowers and fragrant smels doth yeild,
And schorchinge Sommer parcheth corne in feild,
Which Goddes Ceres first to use did bringe.
          Autumnus doth returne with fruits increase,
30   The sturdy stormes in winter seldome cease.

This harmony most temporate doth nourishe
Producinge what in world do live and move:
By death againe it doth the same remove,
Bringinge to nothinge that which late did florish. /
35   Amongst these chaunges God on highe doth reigne,
          Who guidinge reines of thinges dothe them containe. /

Remaininge Kinge and Lord, Fountaine and Springe,
The lawe and prudent Iudge of causes right,
Who doth revoke thinges movinge by his might,
40   And doth to quiet rest their motions bringe. /

So that they cannot in their course endure,
His grace unstable thinges makes to be sure. /

For now unles the souuereigne lord of all
Revokinge should renewe the Worldes progression,
45   *And should theire orbes containe in due succession,*
Declininge things by wisedome to recall:
    The thinges wch stable order now doth swaye,
    Dissolved from theire fountaine, would decay. /

This God is unto all the common love,
50   *And everie creature doth one thinge require,*
To supreme goodnes end for to aspire.
For otherwise they cannot live or move,
    Unlesse with pure love they returne againe
    To sovereigne cause, who doth their state maintaine. /

Prose 7

P. Do you not now apparently behould
What consequentlie may inferred be,
From p[re]mises before, wherof wee spake?
B. What followeth thence? *P.* That all *fortunes* events
5   Undoubtedlie are good. *B.* How can y^t be?
P. Knowe you, whereas all *fortune* sweete and sowre,   48·/[r]
Partlie the godlie to remunerate,
Or them to exercise imposed is. /
And partlie for this end, y^t wicked men
10   Might punishment and due correction beare.
Every event of *fortune good* I deeme,
W^{ch} iust or profitable still doth seeme. /
B. This is, I say a reason passing true. /
And when I call to mynd *Gods providence,*
15   Or fate, wherof you have discoursed late,
This sentence wth firme props supported stands.
But if you please we may associate
This sentence wth them whom you have before
Alleadged, mans opinion to surmount.
20   *P.* Wherefore? *B.* Because the com[m]on phrase of men
Doth oft inculcate this y^t to some folke

Fortune is evill. P. Will you therefore
Y^t wee a litle while examine now
These phrases of the vulgar sort of men?
25   Lest we to much from mans capacitie
May seeme herein reclyninge to digresse.
B. Do as you please. *P.* Do you not that esteeme
W^{ch} profiteth, to be *good*? *B.* Doubtles, yes. /
P. Now y^t wch either exerciseth man,
30   Or doth correct is profitable. *B.* True.
P. Then is all *fortune good*, indeede. *B.* What els?
P. But this is such mens fortune, who are sett
In vertues fortresse, and do warre attempt
Against adversities, or els from vice
35   Declininge, chose the path of vertues all.
B. I can it not deny. *P.* What do you think
Of fortune prosperous, wch in good men
Is granted for a *guerdon*° or reward,
Do common people iudge y^t to be naught?
40   *B.* ffy no, but as it is, they iudge it *good.*
P. What do the people thinke of all the rest
W^{ch} beinge sharpe wth rigor do restraine
The wicked by deserved punishment,
Do they the same esteeme for to be *good*?
45   *B.* Of all things wch may be imagined,
The people iudge this miserable most.
P. Marke then if wee the com[m]on peoples voyce
Thus imytatinge, may not thence conclude   [48 v]
That wch surmounteth mans opinion.
50   *B.* What thinge is that? *P.* From former p[re]mises
Graunted already it will follow right
Y^t all events of *fortune* resteth *good,*
To such as vertue have, or growe therin
Or vertues would atchive. But unto them
55   Who in impietie abide, *fortune* is naught. /
B. This thinge is true, though none dare it confesse. /
P. Why so a wise man ought not much to greive
When he is urg'd wth fortune to contend,
No more then it becomes a valiant man,
60   Wth indignac[i]on to perplex his mynd,

When the *Al-arme*⁵⁰ doth sommon him to warre.
ffor unto both⁵¹ yᵗ difficult turmoyle
Then im[m]inent is cause materiall
Unto the one to propagate his fame
65   Unto the oth[er] wisdome to confirme.
And thereuppon vertue hath got her name,
Because dependinge on her proper strength
By nothinge opposit *she* is subdued.
Nor you who placed are in vertues path
70   Cam to the world to wollow in delights,
And to continue in yo[ur] pleasures vaine,
But warre you wage wᵗʰ fortune of all sorts.
Wherefore lest fortune sorrowfull oppresse,
Or pleasant fortune may yo[ur] mynds corrupt,
75   Wᵗʰ all yo[ur] strength embrace the goulden meane.
ffor whatsoever doth come short thereof
Or els exceedeth it, unhappie is,
And is wᵗʰout reward. ffor in yo[ur] selves
It doth consist what *fortune* you will frame,
80   For every thinge yᵗ seemeth rigorous,
        Good men doth exercise, or els correct,
        Or els it punisheth the wicked sect. /

Metrum 7 ·

Kinge Agamemnon waginge ten yeares warre,
*Troy did ruinate in Phrigia*⁵² *farre:*
Revenginge Paris wronges who had defiled
His brother Menelaus wife beguiled.
5   *When he with Græcian fleete to saile did mynd,*
With bloud he purchased a prosperous wind: 49 ·[r]
Castinge of love wᶜʰ parents exercised,
He let the Preist his daughter sacrifice.
Ulisses did bewaile his losse of men
10   *Whom Poliphemus fierce in hollow den*
Lurkinge, in savage sort did ill entreate,

---

⁵⁰ *Al-arme*] "u" *deleted after* "r" *MS*
⁵¹ both] "o" *deleted after* "o" *MS*
⁵² *Phrigia*] "h" *inserted above with caret*

Devouringe them in gredy paunche⁵³ for meate:
Who sleapinge, yet Ulisses wᵗʰ greife sad
Thrust out that monsters eye with anger mad.
15   Wherby reveng'd on him he did restore
Ioy to his heart, and eies that wept before. /
Labours full difficult of Hercules
Do celebrate his highe renowned praies,
The Centaures proude in strength he did subdue.
20   The Lions skine he stripped and him slue.
The Harpies wᵗʰ his arrowes put to flight.
The goulden apples he did take by might,
Althoughe the Dragon did him then behould,
Yet he did loade his hand with massie gould.
25   Dogge Cerberus wᵗʰ tripple cheine he drew.
The cruel Diomede he overthrewe,
And gave him to his horses beinge deade,
Which wonted were⁵⁴ with mans flesh to be fed.
Revivinge monster Hydra feirce in ire
30   By him was slaine, his venime burn'd with fire.
Achelous ashamèd for his disgrace
Within his banckes hid his deformed face. /
Antaeus,⁵⁵ whom earth did to strength restore,
Lifting from earth, he slue on Libian shore.
35   Fire-spittinge Cacus he did slay in feight,
Whereby Evanders ire aswaged streight.
Those shoulders stronge wᶜʰ skies waight should sustaine,
Th'Arcadian Boare foaminge uppon, was slayne. /
And this of Hercules was labour last,
40   In Atlas steede he bear the heavens vast,
With necke not bowinge. So the skies he wonne,
As guerdon° for the worke which he had done. /
            Ye valiant hartes with might march forward then,
            Folow these statelie steps of worthy men.
45   Why do ye (base mindes),⁵⁶ fainte, abhorringe paines?
            Subdue earthes clogge, and skies shall be yo[ur] gaines.

---

⁵³ paunch] "h" inserted above with caret
⁵⁴ were] "a" deleted after first "e" MS
⁵⁵ Antaeus] Anthous MS
⁵⁶ mindes),] mindes,) MS

THE · PHYSICKE[1] · OF[2] · PHILOSOPHIE[3] ·
compiled by Anicius Manlius Torquatus
Severinus Boethius, touching the
consolation of Lady Philosophy
in the[4] tyme of
his exile · /

The fift booke wherin she resolveth him of certaine
doubts arising from the consideration of Gods
providence touching chaunce and fre-will. /

Prose 1 ·

These words *she* spake, and then of other things
To treate and speake *she* turned her discourse.
Then I thus said, yo[ur] exhortac[i]on
Aptly is framed, and beseemeth best
5   Yo[ur] grave authoritie. But I perceave
Y^t true it is, wch you remembred late,
Y^t the deepe question of *providence*
Intangled is wth many doubts profound. /
ffor I demand whether determine you
10   Y^t chaunce is any thinge? And what chaunce is?
P. My debt late promised to pay, I hast,
And unto thee the way to manyfest,
Whereby to native soyle thou mayest repayre. /
But these thy doubts, thoughe to be understood
15   They profitable are, yet they digresse
A litle from the path of o[ur] intent. /

---

[1] *PHYSICKE*] "C" *inserted above with caret*
[2] *OF*] *inserted above with caret*
[3] *PHILOSOPHIE*] *PHILOSOPIE MS*
[4] the] the *deleted after the MS*

And it is to be feared lest thy *minde*,
In by-pathes intricate long weried,
To find the right way hardlie will suffice. /
20   *B.* That thinge you nothinge neede to feare at all. /
For calme contentments quiet ease it is
For me to understand doubts difficult,
Wherin my *mynd* conceiveth cheife *delight.* /
And when[5] the body of yo[ur] disputac[i]on
25   Shall wholely cleared from all doubts appeare:
Concerninge other things wch may succede
No questions difficult will thence arise. /
P. To[6] thy[7] desire, said *she*, I condiscend.
And therwthall to speake *she* thus began:
30   Yf any man define chaunce in such sort
As if it were *Event* at randome done   50 ·[r]
By headlonge moc[i]on, rashly brought to passe
Wthout all *Causes* certaine *union*,
I then affirme nothinge is *Chaunce* at all. /
35   And do esteeme it as a naked name,
Distinct from true signification
Of *subiect matter* wch we have in hand. /
ffor what place can be left to rash event,
Sith all things *God* doth wiselie keepe in frame. /
40   For true it is y^t nothinge beinge hath
From nothinge, wherto all *antiquity*
Wth one consent ever subscrybed hath. /
Yet this is not a fundamentall ground
Includinge *God* the first creatinge cause:
45   But to materiall subiects doth extend,
Namely to *nature* of created *formes.* /
But if y^t from no causes, any thinge
Beginninge hath, it seemeth to aryse
ffrom nothinge: and if y^t cannot be done,
50   It is impossible y^t there can bee
Such *Chaunce*, as wee before defined late. /
B. How then? Is nothinge to be rightlie cald

---

[5] when] *inserted above with caret*
[6] To] *erasure in MS over-written*
[7] thy] *letter deleted after "h" MS*

By *names* of chaunce or fortunes casuall?
Or is there any thinge, (allthough unknowne
55   Unto the vulgar sort) whereto these names
Conveniently may serve for to expresse?
P. My *Aristotle* in his *physickes* hath
Both[8] breiflie, and accordinge to the truth
This thinge defyned well.[9] *B.* I pray you how?
60   *P.* Whenas a thinge is undertaken for
Som certaine end, if y^t another thinge
Then was intended haply come to passe
Uppon occasion of some other cause:
Y^t same *Event* is nominated *Chaunce.* /
65   As if a man intendinge to manure
His field, and for y^t end digginge the ground
Shall find a masse of gould, then such event
Is thought to fall out by *Chaunce casuall.* /
Yet notwthstandinge this doth not befall
70   From nothinge, but his proper causes hath,
W^{ch} then concurringe by a sodaine hap,
And unexpected, seemes to make the *Chaunce.* /
ffor if the *Tyller* had not dig'd[10] the ground   [50 v]
Or if the owner, had not in y^t place
75   His money hid, the gould had not ben found. /
Then these are causes of such sodaine chaunce,
When any thinge produced comes to passe
From meetinge causes, wch do all concurre
Wthout the doers expectation,
80   Or the intention wherat he did ayme. /
For neither y^t man who had hid the gould
Nor he y^t did the ground manure, did meane
Or in his thoughts intend the mony should
Be found, but as I said, what th'one had hid,
85   It did concurre, and haplie came to passe,
The other should there dig where it was lay'd.
Therfore wee may define *Chaunce* properly
To be, an unexpected workes event

---

[8] Both] "o" *deleted after* "o" *MS*
[9] well] *inserted above with caret*
[10] dig'd] digd *MS*

Procedinge from encountringe causes force,
90   In such things as for other ends are meant. /
But *divine order* wch doth still proceede
Wth an inevitable causes lincke,
Discendinge from *fountaine* of *providence*,
    W^{ch} doth in place and tyme, dispose all things,
95   Causes so to concurre to-gether brings. /

Meter 1 ·

The river Tygres and Euphrates rise
From one Springe, in the craggie Parthian hills,
Where castinge backward darts the souldier flies,
Where with pursuinge enymies he kils. /
5   *This Springe devided streight two chanels fils,*
    Whose streames if afterwards they meete, such thinge
    Must also meete, wch both[11] those rivers bringe

As shipps must needes concurre, and stemmes of trees. /
And though such things do seeme by chaunce to flowe,
10   *Yet rivers banckes guidinge them, maketh these*
To passe alonge what way the streames do go:
And doth direct them in the current lowe. /
    So chaunce, wch seemes to float without all reines,
    Is curbed, whom the lawe of fate restraines. /

Prose 2 · /   51·/[r]
B: These things I well observinge understand
And to yo[ur] speeches I yeild my assent.
But in this firme united causes cheine
Is there no libertie of mans freewill?
5   Or doth this fatall linke of *providence*
The moc[i]ons of all humanine mynds restreine?
P. There is freewill, nor reason naturall
In any creature hath been ever knowne,
But they have had the libertie of will.
10   ffor what thinge naturally reason hath,
The same hath iudgment whereby, every thinge
It may, according as it is, discerne.

---

[11] both] "o" *deleted after* "o" *MS*

Wherfore what thinge is meete to be eschew'd,
And what is to be wished it doth knowe.
15 And what a man doth iudge to be desyred,
He doth require. But he doth y^t eschewe
W^{ch} he thinks fit to be abandoned.
Then in all those in whom doth reason rest
Freedome to will and nill is in theire mynds.
20 But y^t this freedome equall is to all
I do not here affirme for *essences*
W^{ch} are celestiall, and divine, have
Iudgment more sound, and will more incorrupt,
Also abilitie effectuall, ~ ~
25 They have to execute what they desire.
And soules of men must needs be farr more free
When they in contemplac[i]on of *Gods will*
Continue firme, and they are not so free
When they decline unto the bodies base.
30 And yet lesse free they are when passions vayne
Do bynd their acc[i]ons wth an earthlie cheine,
But extreame slavery of soules it is,
When as addicted unto vices foule
They fall away from firme possession
35 Of understandinge proper unto men. /
ffor after y^t theire eyes they shall divert
From beames of perfect truth y^t mounts on highe,
To gaze on things belowe obscure and darke,
Streightway wth mistie clouds of ignorance   [51 v]
40 They blinded are, and wth affections
Pernicious, disturbed they turmoyle.
Whereto when they approach, and give consent,
Their slavish servitude they do augment:
Wherein them *selves* they have¹² enwrapped fast,
45 And in some sort them *selves* do captivate,
And proper libertie do ruinate.
W^{ch} things neverthelesse the sight divine
Of *providence,* from all eternity
Behouldinge, all events doth clearely see,
50 And doth dispose all things p[re]destinate,

---

¹² have] *inserted above with caret*

Accordinge to their merrits severall.
He superviseth all, and heareth all.[13]

Meter 2 ·
Homer wth eloquences streames
Which from him flow mellifluous,
In verse depainteth Phœbus beames
Brightly displayd perspicuous,
5   *Howbeit Sunne is not of might,*
      Into earthes depth to peirce wth light,
      The depth of Sea doth passe his sight,
      Obscured inconspicuous. /

In worldes Creator doth consist
10 *More bright beames, for he vieweth all.*
No masse of earth can him resist,
No gloumy night so darke can fall,
      But in one act his eye of mynd
      What is, was, or shall be doth finde.
15   *Then viewinge sole all thinges in kind,*
      Sole Sunne we may God truly call. /

Prose 3 ·
[*B.*] Se now I am wth ambiguity
More difficult ensnared then before. /
P. What ambiguity? But where wth all
Yo[ur] mynd purplexed standeth I do gesse. /
5 *B.* That *God foreknoweth all* things and events   52·/[r]
Directly seemeth for to contradict
And quite repugneth freewills libertie. /
For if all things, *Gods* wisdome doth foresee,
And by no meanes can be deceaved, then
10 Y^t thinge must necessarilie fall out
W^{ch} *providence* foresawe to come to passe. /
Wherefore if *God* from all *eternitie*
Not only doth fore-knowe mens actions:
But also knowes theire consultac[i]ons,

---

[13] *ll. 51–2: indentation omitted in MS*

15   And inclinac[i]ons of their harts desire.
          Then shall there be no freedome of the will. /
          ffor neither can be any other fact
          Attempted, or another will can stand,
          But such alone as divine *providence*,
20   W^{ch} cannot be deceaved, did *fore-knowe*.
          ffor if *Events* of things could otherwise
          Be wrested, then they are by *God fore-seene*,
          Then *prescience* of *future* things *Events*
          Fixed im[m]utable there should not be,
25   But rather an *opinion* waveringe,
          W^{ch} thinge of *God* once to imagine, were
          Abominable wickednes, I iudge. /
          Neither can I such *sophistrie* approve
          Wherby this questions knott some do believe
30   May be dissolved, for they this affirme:
          Event of things doth not succeede therefore
          Because *Gods providence fore-sawe* the same
          Should be effected. But contrarywise
          Rather, because the thinge should take effect
35   Therfore *Gods providence* cannot thereof
          Be ignorant. But if the case[14] were so,
          This needs declineth to the adverse part.
          For so necessity there should not be
          Y^t things *foresene* should therefore take effect,
40   But a neceßitie should be inferr'd
          Y^t *future thinges Events* should be *fore-seene*. /
          As thoughe the question were what is the cause
          Of both these things: wheth[er] *Gods prescience*
          Do cause necessitie to future things,   [52 v]
45   Or future things doe cause *Gods prescience*. /
          But wee endevo[ur] to make manifest
          Y^t howsoever causes order stand,
          Th'event of things *fore-knowne* must needs succeede, /
          Allthoughe *Gods prescience* to future events
50   Seeme not neceßitie for to inferre. /
          ffor if a man do sitt, th'opinion
          W^{ch} iudgeth him to sitt is certaine true. /

---

[14] case] "u" *deleted after* "a" *MS*

Contrarywise if the opinion
Touchinge a man y^t he doth sitt, be true:
55 It cannot be but such man then doth sitt. /
Then in them both[15] necessitie remaines,
Neceßity to sitt is in the one,
Neceßity of truth is in the other.
But yet a man doth not for this cause sitt,
60 Because the iudgement y^t he sitts is true,
But rather such opinion standeth true,
Because it chaunced that the man did sitt.
And so allthoughe the cause of truth hereof,
Proceedeth only from one part of these,
65 Yet notwthstandinge in both parts there is
Common neceßitie. And in like sort
Concerninge *providence*, and future things,
It is most evident wee may dispute,
ffor thoughe, because *Events* will come to passe
70 *Gods providence* doth therefore them foresee
And not because such things were seene before
Therefore they come to passe. Nevertheles
Neceßity there is y^t things to come
Should be by *God* foreseene, and that such things
75 As are fore-seene should likewise take effect. /
W^{ch} thinge alone sufficeth to destroy
The doctrine of the liberty of will. /
Now how p[re]posterous a thinge is this
Y^t the *Event* of temporall affaires
80 Should be imagined to be the cause
Of *Gods foreknowledge* wch eternall is,
What is it els to thinke, y^t therefore *God*
Fore-seeth future things, because they are   53·/[r]
To come to passe, then to imagine that
85 *Events* wch heretofore were brought to end
Were cause of *Gods highe providence divine*. /
Moreover even as, when I do knowe
A thinge to be, the same thinge *beinge hath*
So when I knowe a thinge shall come to passe
90 The same thinge of necessitie shall come:

---

[15] both] "o" *deleted after* "o" *MS*

So then it followeth by consequent
Non can avoyd *fore-knowne* things accident. /
Lastlie if any man a thinge esteeme
For to be otherwise then the thing is,
95   The same not only is no knowledge sound
But is deceiveable *opinion* false,
From truth of knowledge far distinguished. /
Then if a thinge be so to come to passe
As the *Event* therof uncertaine stands,
100   Nor necessarily doth take effect:
How can such thinge be manifestlie knowne
Before it come y^t it shall sure succeede?
ffor as firme knowledge is not wth falshood
Mixed at all, so y^t wch is thereby
105   Once app[re]hended cannot otherwise
Remaine, then as it app[re]hended is. /
ffor this the reason is why knowledge sound
Hath no untruth therin, because necessitie
Ther is, y^t every thinge should so consist
110   As knowledge comp[re]hendeth it to stand.
What then? How can *God* things to come *fore-knowe*
W^{ch} are uncertaine? For if he account
Y^t such *Events* will come aßuredlie,
Wherof is possibilitie not to come:
115   He is therin deceaved, wch to thinke
Not only is profane, but once to speake. /
But if, as things are, *God* do them behould
That they shall even so be brought to passe
So as he knowe y^t it is possible
120   Such things may take effect, or no effect:
What p[re]science[16] were this, wch doth conceive
No certainetie, nor firme stability?
Or what would such *fore-knowledg* disagree
From speach propheticall ridiculous[17]
125   Of ould *Tyresias*? What-so-ever I   [53 v]
Shall speake will eyther come to passe, or not. /
Yea, what would *divine providence* exceede

---

[16] *p[re]science*] "r" *inserted above*
[17] ridiculous] "o" *inserted above with caret*

Humaine opinion, if, as men, *God* iudge
Such things to be uncertaine, whose *Event*
130   Uncertaine stands? But if nothinge can be
W^th y^t most certaine fountaine of all things
Uncertaine: then the *Event* of things is sure
W^ch he fore-knew im[m]utably to come.
Wherfore no *libertie* at all ther is
135   In humaine counsells, or mans actions
W^ch *divine Intellect* behouldinge all
At once, w^thout *erroneous* falsity,
To one *Event*, doth firme constreine and ty. /
To wch thinge if wee once shall condescend
140   There will greate inconvenience arise
In humaine thinges. For then in vaine wee should
Rewards to *Godly men*, or punishments
Unto the *wicked sort* propound. W^ch things
No free and voluntary moc[i]on
145   Of their mynds hath deserved to receave. /
And of all things y^t should seeme most uniust
W^ch now is iudged to be equall most.
Namely y^t *bad men* should be punished,
Or y^t *good men* should a reward receive. /
150   Whom not their proper will enforced hath
To good or evill, but neceßitie
Of future things fixed, compelled them. /
Neith[er] should *vices* then be any thinge,
Nor *vertues* any thinge, but rather then
155   A mixt and indiscreete confusion
Of all deserts of man would here ensue. /
And nothinge may more vile surmised be
Yf *order* all of things from *providence*
Derived should succeede, and no *free-will*
160   Were in mans consultac[i]ons and attempts. /
So should it come to passe y^t *vices all*
W^ch wee com[m]it may be attributed
To *God*, who is the *Author* of all *good*.
Also therby no reason would appeare
165   To hope, or pray for any thinge we want
For what can any man hope, or desire,
When fatall *order* irrevocable

                                                        54 ·[r]

Uniteth firme all things wch man may have. /
Then y^t only associations league,
170 W^{ch} is betwen men, and *God* should surcease
Namely to hope for good, and to entreat
Of *God* to keepe man from *ill accidents.*
For by the price of prayers humblenes
Reward inestimable of *Gods* grace
175 Wee do obtaine. W^{ch} is the only *meane*
Wherby men may be thought wth *God* to talke.[18]
And to y^t *light* wherto no man can come
Before by prayers supplication
He do obtaine the same, he may aspire. /
180 W^{ch} prayers if they seeme to have no force,
By grauntinge of necessitie of things,
W^{ch} are to come, what meanes then [do][19] we have
Whereby we may be lincked and adheare
Unto the *supreame Govenour* of all?[20]
185   Whereby *mankinde*, as you before did say,
    Disioyned from his *fountaine* would decay. /

Meter 3 ·
What cause discordinge parteth concords cheine?
What God hath set such warres betwene[21] truthes two,
That those wch truth distinct do both containe
Togeth[er][22] ioyned seeme not so to doe?
5   *Betwene[23] true thinges can there no discord be?*
    And do all truthes wthin them selves agree?

Mans mynd oppressed wth his members blinde
Which do the knowledge of the soule bereave,
Coniunctions secreat cannot aptly finde,
10 *Nor can the reason of hard thinges conceave.*

---

[18] talke] "l" *inserted above with caret*
[19] [do]] *emendation to complete the intended question [Latin: . . . quid erit quo summo illi rerum principi conecti atque adhaerere possimus?]*
[20] all?] all. *MS*
[21] betwene] "e" *inserted above with caret after* "n"
[22] Togeth[er]] "r" *inserted above with caret*
[23] Betwene] "e" *inserted above with caret after* "n"

Why then do men[24] *so ardently desire*
Unto concealed knowledge to aspire?

Doth doubtfull minde perceive what it would knowe?
But who will strive to knowe thinges manifest?
15   *But if he knowe it not, why seekes he so*
The thinge, whereof he ignorant doth rest?
Unknowne thinges who can seeke? Where[25] *shall he finde?*
Or beinge founde, who knowes formes beinge blinde?   [54 v]

When soule beheld the thoughts of God most deepe,
20   *Thinges generall and speciall then were knowne:*
But since darke bodies cloudy[26] *did her keepe,*
Her knowledge wholely is not overthrowne.
For still she houldeth knowledge generall,
But hath forgotten much in speciall.

25   *Therfore whoso would knowe the veritie,*
Mans soule here neither understandeth all:
Nor ignorant doth altogether ly,
But doth remember matters generall,
Which she retaininge, striveth more and more
30   *That to the whole she may, lost parts restore. /*

Prose 4 ·
P. This questions doubt concerning *providence*
In auncient tymes hath caused much adoe
And *Marcus Tullius* in his distribuc[i]on
Of *divination* hath wth all his force
5   Sifted this thinge, and of yo[ur] selfe the same
Hath very longe and much ben searched for.
But in no sort by any one of you
This hath wth diligence sufficient,
And soundnes ben decyded hitherto,
10   Of whose obscurity this is the cause,
Y^t the discourse of humaine intellect

---

[24] *men] man MS*
[25] *where] were MS*
[26] *cloudy] inserted above with caret*

To puritie of *divine prescience*
Unable is to mount or penetrate,
W^{ch} if it could by thought be compassed,

15   No ambiguitie would therein rest.
W^{ch} now at last to open and unfould
I will attempt but first I meane to prove
Those doubts wch you have moved, to remove.
ffor first I do demand, why you do thinke

20   Their reason unsufficient who say thus?
That for so much as *divine prescience*
Necessitie to future things to cause
They do not iudge, then neither can they thinke
Y^t *prescience* doth hinder mans *free-will*:

25   For do you frame yo[ur] former arguments
To prove necessity of *future* things,
From any other principle, but this:
Y^t such things as are understood before, /   55 [r]
They cannot alter, but must come to passe?

30   ffor if *fore-knowledge* be not any cause
Of the necessitie of things to come,
W^{ch} thinge before yo[ur] selfe confessed late,
Why then shall voluntary things event
Unto a certaine end constrayned be.

35   ffor to the end you may well understand
What consequents arise, let us put case°
There were no such *fore-knowledge* should things then
W^{ch} from the will proceede, in this respect
Unto neceßitie be subiect? *B*: No.

40   *P*. Againe, let us *Gods prescience* affirme,
But such as causeth no neceßitie
Unto the course of things, the liberty
Of will remayneth sound and absolute
No lesse then it before remayn'd, I thinke. /

45   But you will answere, althoughe *prescience*
Cause not necessitie to future things,
Yet notwthstandinge it doth rest a signe
Y^t neceßarilie things shall be done,
But so allthough *free-knowledge* had not been,

50   Th'*event* of things to come would seeme to be
Effected neceßarily likewise. /

For every signe doth only manyfest
And shewe the thinge whereof it is a signe,
But not effect what it doth represent. /
55   Then this thinge first should demonstrated be
Y^t all things by neceßitie fall out.
Y^t so it may appeare foreknowledge is
A signe^{27} of such necessitie of things. /
For otherwise if there be no such thinge,
60   The other cannot be a signe of that
W^{ch} is not any thinge. / But it is plaine,
Y^t demonstrac[i]on wch supported stands
By reason firme, is not to be deryved
From naked^{28} signes, neith[er] from Arguments
65   Externally deduced but it is
To be produced from convenient
And neceßary causes evidence.
But how can it avoyded be, you say,   [55 v]
Y^t those things w^{ch} *Gods prescience fore-sawe*
70   Would come to passe, should not so take effect?
Allthoughe wee hould what *providence* foresawe
Would come to passe should not accordingly
Effected be, and do not rather thinke,
Y^t thoughe they take effect, neverthelesse
75   In their owne nature, no neceßity
Y^t they should so be brought to end ther was.
W^{ch} you hereby may easily observe.
We, many things obiected to o[ur] eies
While as they are adoinge, do behould.
80   As y^t w^{ch} *Coachman* are beheld to do,
In guidinge and in turninge of their *Coach*.
And such like voluntary acc[i]ons:
Doth then necessity at all constraine
Any such act to be effected?^{29} *B.* No. /
85   For vaine it were to use the helpe of art,
Yf all should, by compulsion, moved be. /
P. Then those *events*, wch when men them attempt

---

^{27} signe] "h" *deleted after* "g" *MS*
^{28} naked] *word deleted with* naked *inserted above with caret*
^{29} effected] *some letters over-written*

Have no necessity, to come to passe:
The same things are wthout neceßitie
90   To take effect, before they come to passe.
Then certaine things to take effect there be
Whose end from all neceßitie is free. /
And this I thinke no man will hence inferre
Y^t those things wch allready take effect
95   Were not to come to passe before they came.
Wherefore the things *fore-knowne* have free *Events*.
ffor as the *knowledge* of things p[re]sent cause
No necessary act, so to *foreknowe*
Events to come doth no neceßity
100   Inferre to things y^t are to come to passe. /
But you alledge this questionable rests
Whether ther can be any *prescience*
Of such things wch contingent do remayne.
For these two things do seeme to disagree,
105   And you suppose if things be knowne before,
They must succeede of mere necessity.
Yf no necessitie there were thereof,
They could not be by any means *fore-knowne*.   56·/[r]
And you thinke nothinge but a certainty
110   Can comp[re]hended be by *prescience*.
And if the thinge whose ends uncertaine stand
Be so fore-sene as if they certaine were,
You iudge that were a doubt^{30} ambiguous,
Distinct from *verity* of knowledge firme.
115   ffor otherwise to make account of things
Then things in *nature* are[,] you do believe[,]
Farr from integrety of knowledge swerves.
The reason of w^{ch} *error* is, because
All things wch any man doth app[re]hend
120   He demeth y^t such things are understood
Only by force and *nature* of the things
W^{ch} he doth knowe, wch wholely is untrue. /
ffor every thinge wch knowledge doth conceive
Is not so^{31} app[re]hended as it is,

---

^{30} a doubt] a doubt *deleted after* a doubt *MS*
^{31} so] *inserted above with caret*

125   Accordinge to the *nature* of it selfe:
        But is accordinge to the faculty
        Of them who knowe the same, rather perceav'd.
        As by this short example may appeare,
        The sight, and touchinge, do in severall sort
130   The selfe same roundnes of a body knowe.
        The one farre of doth viewe the body whole,
        Castinge his beames of *sight* at once thereon.
        The oth[er] doth the roundnes app[re]hend
        By partes therof, when it approacheth neare,
135   Coheringe and environinge the same.
        The sences also do a man p[er]ceive
        After one sort, *Imagination*
        After another sort, *Reason also*
        After anoth[er] manner doth him see.
140   And *divine Intellect* doth otherwise behould. /
        For *sence externall* doth the *shape decerne*
        As it in subiect matter doth consist.
        The *Phantasies imagination*
        Sole *shape abstract* from matter doth behould.
145   *Reason* surmounteth this, consideringe
        In universall sort the *species*
        W^ch is in men perticuler beheld.
        But *eye of Intellect* mounteth more highe   [56 v]
        Above the bounds of universall things,
150   And doth behould wth purest sight of *mynd*,
        The verie formes simplicity in man. /
        Wherin this cheifely may be pondered
        Y^t the superiour meanes of app[re]hension
        Doth the inferio[ur] in it comp[re]hend
155   But the inferio[ur] cannot any way
        Arise to comp[re]hend the higher meanes.
        For outward senses cannot any thinge
        W^thout a subiect matter, app[re]hend,
        Neith[er] *Imagination* doth perceive
160   The universall *species* of things.
        Nor *Reason* can a simple forme conceive,
        But *divine knowledge* viewinge from above,
        Not only doth the forme internall, see,
        But also whatsoever in the same

165   Contayned is, doth fully comp[re]hend.
So as y^t forme, wch by no meanes besides
Can be perceived, it doth understand. /
For both the *Reasons knowledge generall*,
The *figure of imagination*,
170   And[32] matter sensible it doth conceive,
Not usinge *Reasons* helpe, or *phantasie*,
Or outward *sense*, but (as a man would say)
All things, behouldinge formally at once,
In one instant perceivinge of the mind
175   And *Reason* also, when it doth respect
A universall thinge, doth neither use
Helpe of the *Phantasie*, or other sense,
Yet all imaginable things doth knowe.
And things obiected to the outward sence,
180   For it is reason wch in gen[er]all
Defineth things in the discourse conceiv'd,
As thus: *Man is a livinge thinge, wch hath
Only two[33] feete, [and][34] reasons use wthall.*
W^{ch} *definition*, though it manifest
185   A univ[er]sal *notion*, to the *mynd*
Yet *non* is ignorant, y^t this doth showe
And comp[re]hend a thinge imaginable,
And sensible wch reason doth not viewe,   57 ·[r]
By benefit of *phantasie, or sense*,
190   But only by conceivinge *rationall*.
Also the *phantasie* althoughe from the *sense*
Of *sight*, *she* tooke begininge, shapes to frame
Neverthelesse wthout the helpe of *sense*
It doth all matters sensible behould,
195   Not in a sensible respect of *sight*,
But in imaginary sort, therof
Iudginge,[35] and app[re]hendinge what it is.
Then do you not hence plainely understand
Y^t in perceivinge, all things rather use

---

[32] And] nd *inserted above with caret*
[33] *two*] tow MS
[34] [*and*]] *ampersand MS*
[35] Iudging] "g" *inserted above with caret after* "d"

200   Their proper faculty, then of such things
        W^{ch} are perceived. And not wthout iust cause:
        ffor wheras every iudgment is the act
        Of him y^t iudgeth, it behoveth then
                That he should iudge not by externall sight,
205   But should his worke effect by proper might. /

                        Meter 4 ·
        Ould Stoickes in their sentences obscure
        Maintained that representations
        Of things imprinted on mans mynd endure
        Infixing stronge imaginations:
5   *Like as wth pen men write in paper cleane,*
                Which did before no letters shape containe. /

        But if the agent soule nothinge expresse
        By inward motion, but doth patient ly,
        Subiect to shapes wch outward thinges impresse,
10   *As glasse returneth images to eye,*
                From whence doth come such knowledge to the mynd,
                Whose sight surveieth all thinges in their kind?

        What facultie could then peirce into all?
        What faculty things compound could divide?
15   *Or parted thinges to one head could recall?*
        Sometimes both waies thinges lofty to decide,
                Sometimes in speciall to descend belowe,
                Discoursinge till error by truth she showe?   [57 v]

        This mind is far more mightie cause then such
20   *As like materiall thinges, impressions bide:*
        Yet passive force precedent stirreth much,
        And oft mans mind doth unto actions guide.
                Namely when light doth penetrate the eye:
                Or when a voice in eare doth soundinge cry. /

25   *Then stirreth up the action of the mynd,*
        Recallinge species wch she first conceived,
        Like motions framinge, wch she doth in kind
        Apply to outwarde shapes wch she perceived.

Which thinges externall she most aptly mixeth
30   *To inward formes, wch she wthin her fixeth.*

Prose 5

     Now if in bodies app[re]hension,
     Allthoughe obiected outward qualities
     Do penetrate the instruments of *sense,*
     And thoughe the bodies passion doe p[re]vent
5   The vigor of the agent mynd, wch may
     Provoke the action inward of the *mind*
     And so may stirr internall restinge *formes,*
     I say in bodies app[re]hension
     Yf that the *mind* be not wth passion stirr'd,
10   But by his proper facultie do iudge
     The subiect passive bodies moc[i]on:
     Then how much more *Intelligences free*
     Exempted from all bodies, passions,
     In app[re]hension do not imitate
15   Externall obiects, but do exercise
     The only action of internall mynd?
     Then in this manner knowledge manifould
     To distinct *natures* diversely pertaines:
     ffor unto livinge thinges wch do not move
20   From place to place (as shell-fish in the sea
     And oth[er] livinge *Creatures* wch to *rockes*
     Cleaving are nourished) only a *sense*
     Voyd of all other knowledge doth belonge. /
     Imagination doth pertaine to beasts
25   Which move from place to place, in whom to flee,
     And covet things, affections do appeare.   58·/[r]
     Reason to mankind sole doth appertaine
     And sole *intelligence* to things divine. /
     From whence it followeth y^{t} such notion
30   All other knowledge doth surmount and passe,
     W^{ch} by *a naturall* instinct doth knowe
     Not o[n]ly[36] what is proper thereunto,
     But understandeth subiects of the rest. /
     What then if *sense* and *phantasie* contend

---

[36] o[n]ly] "n" *indicated above as abbreviation*

35   Wth the discourse of *reason*, and should say
     That the thing generall w^{ch} *reason* doth
     Suppose to understand is nought at all:
     For that thinge wch is by the *sense* perceived
     Or by *imagination* cannot be
40   A univ[er]sall, but a speciall thinge,
     Then *reasons* iudgment eyther standeth true
     That nothinge should be sensible, or els
     Because *she* knoweth many things to be
     Subiect to *senses*, and *imagination*,
45   *Reasons* conceiving should be merely falsh
     W^{ch} taketh y^t to be a generall thinge
     W^{ch} is but sensible, and singuler.
     To wch things if that *reason* should reply
     Contrarywise that shee doth understand
50   Imaginable things and sensible
     After a univ[er]sall sight of mynd,
     And y^t *sense* and *imagination*,
     To universall knowledge of things generall
     Cannot aspire, because their notion
55   Excedeth not the figures corporall,
     And that in understandinge of hard things
     It is the safest way to credit them
     Whose iudgment is more firme and absolute.
     Now in such strife betwen *reason* and *sense*,
60   Would not all wee (in whom the faculty
     As well of *reason*, as of *phantasie*
     And outward *sense* inheareth) countenance
     Rather the cause of *reason*, then of *sense*.
     Alyke it is, y^t humaine *reason* thinks
65   That *divine knowledge* cannot future things
     Further behould then *reason* can perceive. /
     ffor thus by *reason*, you disputed late: [58 v]
     Yf any things seeme not to have *Events*
     Certaine and necessary, then such things
70   To happen cannot firmely be *fore-known*.
     Then of such things can be noe *prescience*.
     W^{ch} knowledge if wee also should beleive
     In casuall things to be, then everythinge
     Should from necessity be brought to passe.

75   Yf then, as wee do *reasons* use enioy,
        So might wee be partakers of *Gods mind.*
        Like as wee iudge *imagination*
        And *sense*, to *reason* ought to render place,
        So would wee likewise iudge it iustest course
80   Y^t humaine *reason* should it selfe submit
        Unto the *divine notion of Gods mind.* /
        Wherefore so much as poßibly wee can
        Let us erect o[ur] selves unto the toppe
        Of y^t most *highe intelligence in God.*
85   ffor there shall *reason* see, what in it selfe
        It cannot comp[re]hend, that is to say
        How *Gods fore-knowledge*, sure, and definite,
        Behouldeth things whose end uncertaine seemes
        Neither is that opinion waveringe.
90   But is the purity of knowledge highe
            Of *God*, wch cannot comp[re]hended be. /

                        Meter 5 ·

How do the beasts, in a showe verie strangly repugninge, on earth go?
Some forowinge body thrust al alonge seely° crepinge upon dust,
Some fly about soaringe verie highe, and mount wth a swift winge,
Some other only to stand do delight with a foote to the firme land.
5   *Some to the feildes merie move, desolate some only the woods love.*
Albeit in varyinge^37 figure all these keepe their abidinge,
Yet grovelinge hevie face to them all procureth a disgrace. /
Only the man elevateth aloft hautie head wth a greate state,
Whose body mounted aright contemneth basenes of earthes sight.
10   *This figure admonisheth man in whom wary wisedome inhereth,*
That sith alone to the skies bodie thine is erected in apt wyse,
        Thou, wth a mind elevated on highe to the skies, be erected,
        Least that alone body mounted aloft, thy minde be deiected.

                        Prose 6   59·/[r]
        Wherfore because (as it is sayd before)
        What thinge so ever may be understood
        Cannot by nature of it selfe be knowne:

---

³⁷ *varyinge] word over-written in bold*

But as the nature of[38] them who do know
5   Doth comp[re]hend, let us now undertake
(So far as lawfull is for us) to viewe
What is the state of *Gods essence divine*,
That what his knowledge is wee may perceive. /
That *God eternall* is[,] it is agreed
10   Amongst all them who reasonable are.
Then let us see what is *eternitie*,
For y[t] will unto us most plainely showe
Both what his *nature* and his knowledge is. /
Eternitie is whole possession
15   *And perfect state of life w[th]out an end.*
W[ch] may more plaine appeare, if we compare
Therew[th] things temporall. ffor what in tyme
Doth live, it beinge p[re]sent doth proceede
From things forepassed unto things to come,
20   And nothinge is in tyme established
W[ch] can at once together comp[re]hend
The entyre space of his continuinge,
But to the morow hath not yet attayn'd,
And hath already lost the tyme forespent.
25   And truly in the p[re]sent tyme ye live
No longer then in that moment of tyme
W[ch] moveable and transitory stands.
Then what so hath succeßion of tyme,
Allthough the same (as *Aristotle* sayd[39]
30   Concerninge the contynuance[40] of the world)
Never bagan, nor never shall have end.
And thoughe the tyme thereof extended were
W[th] infinite continuance of tyme:
Yet is it not a thinge w[ch] may be thought
35   To be eternall, for it comp[re]hends
Not all at once, allthough the space thereof
Were infinit, for it wanteth yet
The future tymes, w[ch] are not yet transact. /

---

[38] it selfe be knowne: / But as the nature of] *inserted above with caret after* by nature of
[39] sayd] sayd) *MS (a redundant parenthesis emended out)*
[40] contynuance] *altered from* countynance ("u" *after* "o" *deleted with second* "u" *inserted above with caret after second* "n")

Then that wch comp[re]hendeth in *one* act
40 And doth possesse the fullnes all at once
Of life interminable, whereunto [59 v]
No tyme to come is absent, or tyme past
Is vanished, may worthely be sayd
To be *eternal* and most requisit
45 It is, y^t p[re]sent things should him assist
And y^t he should have the infinity
Of tymes progression to be p[re]sent still,
From whence some men concluded have amisse
Who when they heare y^t *Plato* did suppose,
50 This world had no beginnings tyme at all,
Nor should at any tyme be brought to end,
They thinke hereby the world w^{ch} *God* hath made
Wth the *Creator* coeternal were
For it is one thinge to be governed
55 Wth life interminables motion,
W^{ch} *Plato* did unto the world ascribe:
Anoth[er] thinge it is to comp[re]hend
The p[re]sence of interminable life
In one act, wch is manifestly knowne
60 To be the property of *divine mind.* /
Neith[er] ought *God* to seeme more auncient
Then creatures, by the quantitie of tyme,
But rath[er] in respect of property
Of his simplicity of *nature* pure. /
65 ffor moc[i]on infinyte of things in tyme
Doth imytate *Gods* p[re]sentary state
Of life eternal and im[m]ovable,
W^{ch} when it cannot equalize or match,
It fayleth of im[m]utabilytie,
70 And doth decrease from the simplicity
Of *Gods Al-presence*, into quantity
W^{ch} is successively made infinit
Respectinge future and fore-paßed tymes. /
And when it cannot altogith[er] have
75 At once the fulnes of the life of *God*,
Yet herein sith it ceasseth not to be
But in one forme or oth[er] doth abide,
It seemeth in some sort to im[m]ytate

Y^t wch it cannot compasse and fulfill.
80 Bindinge it selfe to p[re]sence in some sorte
Of this small transitory pointe of tyme, [60 r]
W^{ch} for so much as it doth rep[re]sent
Certaine simylytude of *Gods presence*
W^{ch} doth eternally fixed remaine,
85 It doth performe to them who have such state
Y^t they to have a^{41} *beinge* may appeare.
But for so much as it could not persist
It tooke the infinit pathway of them,
Wherby it comes to passe it doth prolonge
90 The life procedinge by succession,
Whose plenitude it could not comp[re]hend
By stable permanence im[m]ovable.
Then if we (followinge *Plato*) would impose
Convenient names to things, wee may affirme
95 Y^t *God eternall* is, and y^t the world
Perpetually doth move. Then for as much
As every *iudgment* comp[re]hendeth things
W^{ch} therto subiect are, accordinge to
The *nature* of the thinge wch doth perceive
100 And sith *eternall and All-present state*
In Gods pure nature allwaies doth consist
His knowledge then, wch doth tymes moc[i]on
Exceede, remayneth in the singlenes
Of his owne p[re]sence, and doth comp[re]hend
105 The spaces infinit of tyme forepast,
And tyme to come, and understandeth all
In the *simplicitie* of knowledge his,
As though they were now done in p[re]sent tyme.
Wherfore if you *Gods prescience* perpend,°
110 By wch he understandeth everythinge:
You will not call it *prescience* of things,
W^{ch} are to come, but rather estimate
The same to be, an instant knowledge firme
W^{ch} never fadeth, nor doth passe away. /
115 ffrom whence it is not called *previdence*,
But rath[er] *providence* of *God*: because

---

^{41} a] *inserted above with caret*

It beinge farre remote from lowest things,
Behouldeth *all* from highest toppe of *all*.
Why then do you require that future things
120 Should of *necessitie* be brought to passe?
Because they be in *Gods sight* manifest? [60 v]
For men cause not neceßity to things
W^{ch} they behould: for what you p[re]sent see
Doth yo[ur] sight add thereto necessity?
125 *B.* No, in no sort. *P.* But if comparison
May worthely be made, betwen *Gods* sight
Of p[re]sent things, and sight of mortall man
As you see things in p[re]sent temporall
So he behouldeth all by endles sight.
130 Then this *divine fore-knowledge* chaungeth not
The *nature* and the *propertie* of things,
But doth them see so present in his sight
As they in tyme to come shall still proceede. /
Neither⁴² doth he things *iudgement* so confound
135 But in one instant sight of *mind divine*
Both necessary, and contingent things
W^{ch} are to come he doth discerning knowe:
Like as when you in one instant behould
A man to walke on earth, and sunne in *skie*
140 To ryse, although you both at once behould,
Yet you distinguish them, and do esteeme
The one to be a voluntary act,
The oth[er] necessarylie to come. /
So then the sight of *God* behoulding all
145 Doth not the quality of things disturbe,
W^{ch} things are p[re]sent in respect of him,
But in respect of tymes succession
They are to come in seasons severall.
Whereby it followeth by consequent
150 Y^t this is not *Gods* bare opinion,
But knowledge grounded on undoubted truth
When as he knoweth any thinge shall be,
He cannot be therof, y^t it doth want
Necessity of beinge, ignorant.

---

⁴² Neither] Nether *MS*

155   Here, if you say, the thinge wch God doth see
       Shall come to passe, cannot but have *event*,
       And y^t wch cannot chuse but take effect
       Y^t falleth out of meere necessity,
       And if you urge me to this verie word
160   *Necessitie*, I will acknowledge then
       A thinge wch doth most solid truth containe,   [61 r]
       And hardlie any man will yeild therto
       Consent, or can the same attaine to knowe,
       But he that doth *Gods essence* contemplate.
165   For I will answere thus, the thinge to come
       When you *Gods divine knowledge* do respect,
       Is necessarilie to take effect:
       But when the same thinge is considered
       Accordinge to the *nature* of it selfe,
170   It seemeth free, and altogither voyd
       Exempted from necessitie of fate. /
       For two kinds of necessitie there are
       The first is simple, as necessitie
       There is, y^t every man should mortall be,
175   The other kind is by condic[i]on firme,
       As if you knowe that any man doth walke,
       Y^t he doth walke is a necessitie.
       ffor what a man doth understand to be,
       Cannot be otherwise then it is knowne.
180   But this necessitie condic[i]onall,
       Simple necessitie doth not infere,
       For not the prop[er] *nature* of the thinge
       But the addic[i]on of condic[i]on
       Is only cause of such necessitie.
185   For no *necessitie* constreyneth man
       To walke, who voluntarily doth goe.
       Allthough when he doth walke it cannot chuse
       But of *necessitie* he needs must walke. /
       Then in like manner if *Gods providence*
190   Behouldeth any thinge, in p[re]sent act
       Of *sight*, the same is of *necessitie*,
       Though no *necessitie* at all therof
       In *nature* prop[er] can therto belonge.
       But *God*, those future things wch do proceede

195   From liberty of will, behouldeth all
        As if they p[re]sent were in action
        Then to the sight of *God*, these things referr'd
        Be neceßary, by⁴³ condic[i]on
        Of *Gods All-seeing knowledge*, otherwise
200   Yf by themselves they be considered
        They do not leave their freedome absolute,
        W^ch doth in *nature* unto them belonge. /   [61 v]
        Wherfore undoubtedly all things succeede
        W^ch *God fore-knoweth* to be brought to passe.
205   But from *fre-will* some things thereof procccde,
        W^ch things allthough they do fall out, and be
        In tyme effected, yet the property
        Of *nature*, they thereby do not forgoe. /
        Because, before such things did take effect,
210   It might have ben they had not come to passe.
        But what are wee the nearer if these things
        Be made unneceßary, sith they are
        To come to passe, but the condic[i]on
        Of *divine knowledge*, in every respect
215   As though they were of mere necessity. /
        Herin this difference is betwen these things
        As is betwen the things forenamed late
        Namely the rising *Sunne*, and walking man,
        W^ch acc[i]ons the while y^t they be done
220   They cannot chuse but needs they must be done.⁴⁴ /
        Yet not w^thstandinge, one of them, before
        It came to passe, was of necessitie
        To take effect: the other was not so: /
        So likewise what *God* hath before his eies,
225   W^thout all controversie *beinge* hath
        But of those things, some do descend and springe
        From the necessitie of things by kind,
        Others descend from agents facultie.
        Then not w^thout just cause, wee said before
230   Yf these *events* have a relac[i]on
        To *Gods all-seeing knowledg*, then they are

---

⁴³ by] the *deleted after* by MS
⁴⁴ They cannot . . . be done.] *interlineated*

Things necessary: But considered
Accordinge to the *nature* of them selves
They are exempted from constreyning bounds
235   Of all *necessitie*. As everythinge
W^ch to externall senses doth appeare
Yf you the same to *reason* do referre
It universall is, yf you respect
The *outward senses*, it is singuler. /
240   But you will say if it be in my power
To alter my intents and purposes
I shall make frustrate *divine providence*
When I perhaps shall chaunge what he *fore-knew*. /
I answere you may alter yo[ur] intent   [62 r]
245   But for as much as p[re]sent certainety
Of *providence*, wch cannot be deceav'd,
Behouldeth both how you can chaunge yo[ur] mynd,
And also wheth[er] you chaunge yo[ur] intent,
Or to what act yo[ur] purpose altereth,
250   You cannot *divine prescience* avoyd.
Like as you cannot flee the p[re]sent sight
Of the behouldinge eye of man, althoughe
You chaunge yo[ur] selfe to sundry actions
Farre differinge, by liberty of will. /
255   What then will you reply shall it be said
Y^t *divine understandinge* altereth
After my chaunginge *disposition*,
That when I shall desire, now this, now that,
It seemes to chaunge his course of knowinge? No. /
260   For sight of *God* p[re]vents all future things,
And doth compell and revocate the same
Unto the^45 presence of his knowledge firme.
Neith[er] doth he so chaunge as you surmise
His courses for to knowe nowe this, now that
265   But in a moment, thy mutations
He permanent doth view, and comp[re]hend:
W^ch p[re]sence, all to comp[re]hend and see,
God hath not from *events* of *future* things,
But from his *essences simplicitie*.

---

^45 the] "e" *deleted after* "e" *MS*

270   From whence y^t doubt is also answered,

W^{ch} you not longe before propounded have.

Namely, it were no small *indignitie*,

Yf *future* things wch mortall men effect

Should be affirmed to administer

275   Or be the cause of *knowledge* firme of *God*. /

For this effectuall vertue of *science*

By p[re]sent noc[i]on understandinge all,

Doth unto all their order constitute,

And is not bound unto inferior meanes. /

280   W^{ch} things thus standinge, liberty of will

Doth unto mortall men stable remayne.

Neith[er] do laws wthout iust cause propound

Rewards and punishments unto mens wills,

W^{ch} freed are from all necessity.

285   There is also a *God fore-knowing all*   [62 v]

Who from above behouldeth every thinge. /

And his *All*[-]*present* sight's *eternitie*,

Concurreth wth the future quality

Of o[ur] attempts, distributinge rewards

290   Unto the *good*, and punishments to *bad*.

Neither in vaine is hope[46] fixed in *God*,

Nor praie[rs] vaine, wch when they are aright

Framed, they cannot uneffectuall

Returne in vaine, wherfore abandon vice,[47]

295   Vertues embrace, to right hope lift your mynd,

Humble petic[i]ons direct on highe.

No small necessitie on you is lay'd

(Unles you will dissemble) to retaine

A sincere life, because before the eies

300   Of *God* the *Iudge* you worke, who all descries.° /

Finis Lib: ult.

[*flourish*]

---

[46] hope] "o" *deleted after* "o" *MS*

[47] wherfore abandon vice] wch when they are aright *deleted with* wherfore abandon vice *inserted above with caret after* vaine

Appendix I

Bracegirdle's Metrical Forms[1]

METER	STANZA/RHYME	METRICS
	Book I	
1	couplets	quantitative meter
2	ottava rima *abababcc*	pentameter
3	quatrains *abab*	pentameter
4	heroic couplets	pentameter
5	nonce stanzas [decastich] $a^5b^5a^5b^5c^5c^5d^3e^2d^3e^2$	variable length[2]
6	quatrains *abba*	pentameter
7	nonce stanza *ab throughout*	tetrameter
	Book II	
1	heroic couplets	pentameter
2	nonce stanzas $a^5a^5b^6b^3a^2$ (with interlaced rhymes)	variable length
3	sestets $a^2b^3c^2a^2b^3c^2$	variable length
4	sestets *ababcc*	hexameter
5	rispetto [heroic] *ababccdd*	pentameter
6	sestets *abbaab*	pentameter
7	unrhymed [stichic]	quantitative meter
8	sestets [sextilla] *aabccb*	pentameter

---

[1] See Lewis Turco, *The New Book of Forms* (London: University Press of New England, 1986). See also Alex Preminger and T.V.F. Brogan, *The New Princeton Encyclopedia of Poetry and Poetics* (Princeton: Princeton University Press, 1993).

[2] Superscripted numbers denote the metrical feet per line, indicating more specifically Bracegirdle's sometimes complex poetic structures.

Book III

1	nonce stanzas [decastich] $a^2b^2c^2d^2a^2b^2c^2d^2e^4e^4$	variable length
2	quatrains *abba*	pentameter
3	sestets $a^2b^3c^3a^2b^3c^3$	variable length
4	sestets [sextilla] *aabccb*	pentameter
5	nonce stanzas $a^3a^3a^3b^2c^3c^3c^3b^2d^3d^3d^3b^2$	variable length
6	sestets *ababcc*	tetrameter
7	quatrains $a^4b^2c^4b^2$ *(with internal rhymes)*	variable length
8	nonce stanza *ababcdcdefefgg* *(sonnet form)*	hexameter
9	nonce stanza *ababbcc* *(rime royal form)*	hexameter
10	sestets *ababcc*	pentameter
11	ottava rima *ababábcc*	pentameter
12	quatrains $a^5b^2a^5b^2$	variable length

Book IV

1	quatrains *abab*	tetrameter
2	nonce stanzas [decastich] $a^5b^5a^5b^5c^5c^5d^2e^3d^2e^3$	variable length
3	ottava rima *ababábcc*	pentameter
4	sestets *ababcc*	pentameter
5	sestets *ababcc*	pentameter
6	sestets *abbacc*	pentameter
7	heroic couplets	pentameter

Book V

1	rime royal *ababbcc*	pentameter
2	octaves *ababcccb*	tetrameter
3	sestets *ababcc*	pentameter
4	sestets *ababcc*	pentameter
5	thirteen lines [stichic] *(internal rhyme & final couplet)*	quantitative meter

Appendix II

Selective Glossary

bewray: reveal, betray
    (I, p.5, 1; I, p.5, 7; II, p.6, 43; II, p.6, 96)
brage: boast
    (II, p.7, 103)
carkinge: fretting
    (III, m.3, 13)
descrie: espy, make out, discover
    (I, m.7, 42, V, p.6, 300)
disgraded: formally deposed from a higher rank
    (II, p.4, 46)
echins: urchins
    (III, m.8, 7)
guerdon: reward
    (I, p.4, 21; IV, p.1, 46; IV, p.3, 11; IV, p.3, 16; IV, p.3, 24;
    IV, p.3, 49; IV, p.7, 38; IV, m.7, 42)
jar (iar): jaring, clashing
    (II, m.8, 8)
lowringe: sinking, making low
    (I, m.3, 7; II, p.3, 49)
lucre: financial gain
    (I, p.4, 45)
maugre: in spite of
    (I, m.5, 49)
nice (nicenes): foolishness
    (II, p.4, 49; II, p.4, 71; II, p.6, 23)
packe: leave
    (I, p.4, 75)
perpend: ponder
    (V, p.6, 9)

perspicuous: clear, evident
 (IV, p.4, 158)
pickthanke: flatterer, tale-bearer
 (III, p.4, 17)
put case: let us suppose that
 (II, p.7, 109; V, p.4, 36)
scænicall: illusory, theatrical
 (I, p.1, 33)
sely (seely): miserable, pitiable
 (I, p.1, 8; II, m.7, 12; III, m.8, 1; IV, p.2 174; V, m.5, 2)
suborned: procured unlawfully, purjured
 (I, p.4, 67)
surprice: surpress, take away
 (II, p.4, 107)
tertian ague: a fever of three days
 (III, p.8, 39)
wayne: cart
 (IV, m.5, 5)